Live
Wide
Open

Karen Porter and Kim Ledford

May you continue
to light your light
shine through
Dustin's story.

Kim Ledford
II Timothy 1:7

DEDICATION

We dedicate this book to Dustin.

CONTENTS

ACKNOWLEDGMENTS

Kim would like to express her gratitude to her husband Danny Ledford whose, love, kindness, and patience transcends all. Thanks to Linda McConnell who spent painstaking hours editing our work, Orena Mital Ford for her loving encouragement and beautiful poetry, Sherry North, Debby Mainor, for their support and love. Michael and Julie Aseron, the owners of Shane's Rib Shack in Cleveland, Tennessee for the countless hours spent establishing the Dustin Ledford Scholarship Foundation. Karen would like to thank Nancy Perry, Robert Perry, Maria Cody, Pat Ashton, Anne Lawrence and Kathrine Arrata Lyndes who provided support, talking things over, reading, writing, offering comments, all of which gave her special insight. Pastor Allan Lovelace, and Father Richard Pelky for their many words of spiritual insight and encouragement, and Waterville Baptist Church for their prayers, support and presence through thick and thin. Jim and Christi Porter, who supported and encouraged us. The Writers Alliance of Gainesville for their help moving through the publication process. Last and not least: We beg forgiveness of all those who have helped us over the course of the years and whose names we have failed to mention.

1 PROLOGUE

Dare to look up to God and say, "make use of me for the future as thou wilt. I am of the same mind; I am one with thee. Lead me wither thou wilt. Clothe me in whatever dress thou wilt. -Chapter xci Epictetus

It has been said that we do not remember our lives in years, months, or even days. We remember in small fleeting moments. Sometimes these moments create an atmosphere where a special moment in time seems to last a lifetime. There is no telling who you are going to meet at a KOA. A place that seemed so ordinary is illuminated by the people there. Was it Sandy Tufts who was so nice on the phone when I called for reservations that created that special moment? The Sweetwater Tennessee KOA campground is a great spot to stay. They just want to make everyone feel at home. Maybe it was the beauty of the surrounding pine grove, and that cool summer evening that let Kim and I partake in a special slice of time that would open the way for a story to be shared. Perhaps it was the place that opened a heart to listen. I asked God for guidance with my writing. The path was set before me as the way opened to reveal this story that would enlighten some heavy hearts. The story retold became Dustin's story for others that will take you on the journey of the life of a special man who has made a big impact on so many people's lives.

I met Kim by chance at a KOA. It started the telling of this story. I was just looking for an overnight stop on my way from Florida to Ohio. Kim was taking her husband and granddaughter and three Yorkshire Terriers on a much needed vacation for Father's Day weekend. The camping cabin site my daughter and I stayed in was so very clean and charming. It was the kind of setting that made you wish you stayed longer and none of the children ever wanted to leave. After I registered my camping cabin for the night, my daughter, Christi, picked up the buckets in the water war fun recreation area. She walked across the field and locked eyes with me, her opponent, who was tiredly accepting the role. I was reluctantly grabbing a bucket to retaliate, after the long car trip. Christi laughed, grabbed a bucket of water and shouted "Friend or foe this is no laughing matter." Christi directly hurled the water balloons at me. I grabbed another bucket and threw them back to her. I took a seat on a bench nearby, never losing eye contact with Christi and mouthed the words 'prepare to lose.' The battle had begun and balloon shrapnel along with gallons of water were everywhere. There were balloon catapults and buckets where they could fill their ammunition. The cool balloons splashing on my hot skin was sort of a relief from the ride, but I was getting tired. She said "O.K. o.k. I am getting tired now. You go play over there with those kids while I rest under this tree."

There was the jumping pillow. It was like a trampoline but low to the ground and safer. Christi jumped on that for a while, and the other kids were called to dinner. So we walked past the volleyball and basketball courts, then the playground and finally settled on swimming in the pool quietly. Anyone leaving on a Friday was sad because they wanted to stay and paint the ceramic bears that Mr. Tufts had made for the children in the campsite to make for their dads for father's day. It was less than a mile off the interstate but had no road noise. It was one of those rare treasures you find that is family friendly and clean. The showers were clean and had great pressure along with hot water. Two girls bounced on the bounce pillow for a while, climbed on the monkey bars, and looked through the store.

Christi looked weary of traveling and you could tell she was tired of being with her me all day long and so she prayed she would have a friend to play with in the pool. Her prayers were answered. She became fast friends with another girl close to her age who had just joined her. Serenity swam happily with her. Soon Serenity was called to dinner and they did not want to part. So, an invitation to dinner was extended. Christi and I found myself sitting down eating with a very nice family after a long days drive. Serenity's grandma unfolded her red checkered table cloth onto the picnic table and served us hot dogs and potato chips. A feast for me who had just driven eight hours from Florida, and did not feel like cooking.

Kim, her granddaughter Serenity, and husband Danny, and Christi and I, sat down for dinner together. The Tennessee family was much better equipped with an RV. We were staying in a camping cabin with our Prius. It was father's day weekend. I wondered where their children were. Were they on their way? After all it was only Friday. The sun set and they began to talk as if time was now endless as it always seems when you go camping. Soon I found out that Kim and Danny's son was on his way traveling, but to a different destination than one could ever bring oneself to imagine.

The girls danced in the dark with about eight or nine other kids on the beautifully manicured lawn. They were catching fireflies and putting them in jars. Each child was in awe of their special natural light. You could hear a distant parent saying "You can admire them, but you have to let them go! They belong to God."

Kim went on to explain what journey her son Dustin had undertaken. I breathed in the evening beginnings of mountain air that Florida folk are in such awe of. The fireflies danced in front of them in their show of light. The light of the story was impressed upon my heart and I knew it needed to be told again. Would the light of this story simply fly away like the fireflies of summer? His mother's story and his father's story danced through the pages of my journal shared again and again, taken in, and let go, given and received, just like the fireflies that night.

It was a long story that started about thirty years ago on October 15 1985 a day that could be described as miraculous. Dustin was first held by his mother and father on the day he was born. This in and of itself was a miracle. But, the miracles kept happening. They rejoiced at his new life in their arms. Kim and Danny looked into their son's eyes. This was their child. In fact he was a child of God's. The mosquitos started to bite. It was time to go in. I exchanged addresses. Through prayer I felt a leading opening a way to that very special place so that Dustin's story could be shared. Their story began when they turned to God.

1 A RUDE AWAKENING

Or ever the silver cord be loosed, or the golden bowl be broken, or the pitcher be broken at the fountain, or the wheel be broken at the cistern.
   Ecclesiastes 12:6

Life was like a cherished dream for Kim in the early 70's. She was just twelve. The world opened up to her. Freedoms were being re-examined, questioned and redefined. Change was in the wind with force even in Cleveland, Tennessee. The world was more and more connected. Skylab was launched. Secretariat won the Triple Crown. The Supreme Court overturned states' rights to ban abortion in the famous Roe vs Wade case. The world around Kim was struggling with the boundaries of morality, and the Watergate hearings had begun.

Like the culture of the seventies, Kim was a force in nature that pressed upon boundaries. She demanded what she wanted and got it from her two doting parents. She was a child who knew her own mind. When Kim first started Kindergarten, her mother would bring her two dresses to wear and she would always choose the dress that her mother did not want. She was a willful child. Kim was the baby of four girls. Some said she was spoiled rotten.

Her parents had worked together to please her. She missed her older sisters' giggling and happy presence. She missed watching them put on their make-up and style their hair. Debby was in college in Nashville. Linda was in Montana. She was married and mothering her two children. Sherry was married and raising a two year old and lived nearby in Cleveland. Kim was the only sibling still at home. There were fleeting instants when she felt lonely, but her daddy always seemed to make it up to her. At Christmas she got everything she asked Santa for. She even got an Easy Bake Oven! When Daddy came home from his day of hard work in the construction business, she was the first to meet him at the door. She was proud of the houses he built and loved to laugh and joke with him and ask him how his day went.

The panoramic views in those parts of Tennessee were magnificent and vacationers as well as townsfolk were building homes. Her father always had plenty of work. People came from far and wide just to see the scenic overlooks and breathtaking views. Some of those visitors decided to stay. Everyone loved all that nature had to offer there. The forest, and rivers and fresh air were enticing. Tourists would sometimes come to poke around the hollows and try their hand at rafting if they were adventurous. Even when Kim was young they still had Cragmiles Opera Hall. It was an up and coming town. It was not too small of a town like Lenoir City that still had laws on their books like, "When you pull up to a stop sign you must fire a gun out the window to warn horse carriages that you are coming. In the 1960's, when Kim was born, the population was shy of 16,200 people by four. Cleveland grew to over 23,008 people by 1973.

1973 got off to a good start for so many of us. The Miami Dolphins defeated the Redskins 14 to 7 in the Super Bowl with their first perfect season ever. The world was united by its first worldwide telecast of an Elvis concert in Hawaii. It was an exciting time to be alive. Kim felt secure. She grew up in the same town, with the same parents, and family around her. Kim felt protected from the ever changing world as she sat with her family to enjoy the evening news. Walter Cronkite announced that President Nixon had reached a peace accord in Vietnam. Maybe his promise to end the war would be honored. They all went to bed to continue their sweet dreams. The Vietnam War might be over. Hope and possibility filled her innocent childlike heart as she kissed her father and mother goodnight and went to bed. Her life had been a dream up until now.

Kim's hopeful dream of infinite possibilities exploded. There was a loud noise echoing in her dreams the evening of January 25, 1973. Suddenly screaming awakened her from a gentle tender sleep. Being daddy's little girl became a lost dream. Now she was awakened from that dream. That dream of being with a family with a mom and a dad forever was gone. In her eyes at the time she felt entitled to all the joys and love the world bestowed on her. This too turned out to be just a dream. Right then and there she felt entitled to have her father alive. Unfortunately, she would not be granted that entitlement. Before her father died there was extra love to go around now that all her sisters were out of the house. Daddy's presence was just a dream now. She would awaken to be what she felt so strongly. She now felt like an orphan alone, overnight.

Even though the family came to be at her side, it seemed like one of the loneliest days of her life. It was almost unreal. She replayed the moment in her mind. She pinched herself to make sure this was really happening. Kim remembered she went in her parent's bedroom to see what it was. Mama had called an ambulance. She stumbled in the dark and went to turn all the lights on. She went to her mother's bedroom and saw that her father had had a heart attack. He was on the bedroom floor. She had to go down stairs to wait for the Emergency Medical Technicians and called the family to come to the hospital. She called her uncle and sister in Cleveland. Her daddy had just died in front of her when she was twelve years old.

She stepped into new shoes that just hours ago were little girl shoes with notions of the possible futures she would have with her father, sizing up her dates in high school or to the prom, attending her graduations, recitals, performances, and walking her down the aisle to marry one day. In that instant these possible futures were gone. She came into her parent's bedroom watching her mother trying to perform C.P.R. on her father's lifeless body on the floor.

That first gaze she took at him froze her heart for an instant. It was as if time stood still. Then something shifted inside of her and she was able to move on. The new shoes she stepped into would take her on a walk through emotions too new that only an adult should have to bear. She became an emotionally worn adult overnight. There in the living room, sitting on the couch, holding the phone tightly in her still small hands was a twelve year old girl waiting for EMS and notifying family what had happened. Her father did not revive. The family came after he had been taken to the hospital. Sisters, and nieces, and nephews, uncles, aunts, mothers and daughters held hands and mourned together at the funeral. Kim's young heart was so pained. Her plans had to be changed. In her dream she was ready to test adolescent belligerence on her parents who maintained a loving resilience under all circumstances. This parental safety net was now broken. How could she move on with her life?

Then shall the dust return to the earth as it was" and the spirit shall return unto God who gave it.
Ecclesiastes 7: 7

The grieving process presents itself differently in a young person's life. An older person has a memory of life before a tragedy. A younger person can get the experience fused into their wiring of what makes them an adult. Sometimes that makes them more resilient. Sometimes they make poor choices along the way to fill the empty holes. The grief works its way into a young person's life and leaves them changed. Sigmund Freud aptly said "We find a place for what we lose. Although we know that after such a loss the acute stage of mourning will subside, we also know that we shall remain inconsolable and will never find a substitute. No matter what may fill the gap, even if it be filled completely, it nevertheless remains something else." Kim might have always been looking to fill that empty place throughout her teen years.

Things were different now. God had called her father's spirit home. She was left in dust making her own way new. Her mother's love was with her through anything bad or good, but she too was grieving and needed support. She always remembered the funeral so vividly in her mind. The visiting hours were over. Her mother, herself, and her three sisters sat almost slumped over in chairs all around. They were exhausted from grief and all had tissues held in their hands from hours of crying. Their mother gathered them all at the casket to sing the song 'God Is So Good'. They all sang it. She did not understand why until years later that it was for her mother to teach them how

God carries you through and continues to carry you through life no matter what.

Kim was still wrestling with her grief. That didn't stop her rebellious nature. Perhaps she was looking for the love she lost, when she lost her father. Perhaps she was her usual rebellious self who was trying to show everyone she knew best. When her older boyfriend gave her so much of that attention she lost, she didn't turn it down. She made some wrong choices. At sixteen she was seriously dating a man four years older than she was. He was going to a junior college. She was a junior in high school. She and her friends were mostly talking about whether Han Solo, or Luke Skywalker was the cutest character in Star Wars. They stretched their patience by waiting in line to see 'Star Wars'. The lines were so long that you had to get there early for tickets. Going to see Star Wars, and other movies gave her a sense of support and brought her spirits up. This support did not replace her father's love. Kim was learning that no matter how hard she tried to fill those empty spaces grief bored into her heart, she had to sit with her grief and let it heal over time.

Her boyfriend impressed her with his talk about college and his big fancy words. He had a car that took them on adventures to escape her sadness.

He shaved daily and appeared full grown and mature! He charmed her by opening the door and bringing her flowers. He took her places she wanted to go. He gave her attention she felt she needed. That gap was filled for a little while. She did not think about the choices she made or the consequences of her actions at that moment. She felt she was just beginning to rise above the grief she felt from the loss of her father. She had little discernment, and her father's discernment was painfully absent.

January first of that year was very special to the family. Kim's mother decided that she would remarry. She picked New Year's day as their special day because she felt it was a marker of new beginnings. The groom had lost his spouse. The bride had lost her spouse. Side by side they blended two families and would move on with new lives together. It was a time of renewal and much happiness for them. However, month after her mother was married Kim was pregnant and did not know it.

Meanwhile, Kim was prescribed steroids for her symptoms of mono. The corticosteroids reduced her swelling of the throat, but did not seem to decrease the overall length and severity of the illness as they had hoped. She knew she felt differently, but she did not know why. She was so tired that she had to have home bound instruction. It was her Junior year in high school and there were a lot of assignments. One day she got up enough strength to go to the mall and she was so hungry. She went to a little vendor in the food court called Karmel Korn. She was ravenously hungry. She ate a big fat pretzel and a large tea which made her terribly sick. She would never eat freshly baked bread again. She was getting fewer calls from her boyfriend, because he could not take her out, now that she was ill. Her mother took her to the doctor in the middle of June. She knew there was something more wrong with her. She just had to find out what it was.

The doctor respectfully and kindly broke it to Kim that she had some choices to make that day. The presence of Daddy's love would never leave, but his attention was gone. She yearned for it again. She felt so sad and alone again as she felt her boyfriend started to lose interest. He was not as attentive as before now that she had mono and was home resting so much. Again that empty space was felt. Her father's warm embrace, kind words, and gifts he showered her with were all dissolved into air. It was as if they had turned to dust and returned to the earth with him.

Her mother sat in a chair and the doctor looked over his spectacles at her with raised eyebrows. Kim was pregnant. The shock of this announcement took her to a new low she had never felt before. The doctor was both compassionate and supportive of her as she knew her father would have been. He was a friend of her father's. Her father had built a house for him. He remembered what a wonderful man her father had been whom she had lost too soon. He felt compassion for her condition. Her father's deeds while on this earth had not gone unnoticed. The extension of his love for her was remembered in a doctor's office as she sat on a cold examination table. This doctor took extra special care of her in such a kind manner. He explained to her that she was four and a half months pregnant. She had to make some quick decisions. She could get married, put the baby up for adoption, raise the baby as a single mother, or have an abortion and no one would ever know. There wouldn't be the humiliation of having to go through life a single mother. Her boyfriend was four years older than her. He kept going back and forth contemplating whether or not he wanted to be married. He seemed more interested in the fact that Space Mountain had just opened at Disney World. One minute he wanted to get married. One minute he didn't.

Wise beyond her years she knew she didn't want to bring a young tender soul into this world as a single mother. The father of this child was not mature himself. Right away she knew she was not going to have an abortion. She knew in her heart that abortion would be wrong. Her headstrong nature proved helpful that day. Kim knew it would be best to let another family take care of the baby girl inside of her. Adoption would give her the family and opportunities that Kim could not give her. She had to be strong to do this, but she knew it was the best thing to do for the child. She chose a Baptist Children's home in New Orleans to place her baby girl.

Did she recognize the first moment her little baby came to be? What gave her the strength to realize this little soul was the first of her kind? The miracle that never before was there such a child as this born awakens every heart when it is opened to see this. Each of us is so different and the product of love of two others coming together. That first sound her baby made touched her heart. She could not care for the child that came from her womb. This pained her. Glory rested on Kim when she recognized her ability to mother and carry that baby full term to grace the earth with her life breath. The pain was so deep when she had her eyes so fixed on the baby as she held her in her arms. She had brought this little girl into the world. A part of her heart had to be closed off for the time being to let her baby go when all she wanted was to hold her in her arms. It was a moment of majesty when grace was ushered in. Mercy took its rightful place in Kim's heart when she gave up her new daughter, to this child's new mother who would raise her. It was as if God took this baby seed of life and decided where it needed to be planted. The Holy Spirit moved again in her life when God would wipe her tears of sadness and turn them into joy. Right now she forced herself to celebrate the joy of this new life along with the pain of letting her baby go.

She felt the life inside of her and it dawned on her that this life that grew inside of her was a child of God just as she was. She had been raised in a Christian home and knew that she was carrying a life inside of her that was given by God. The baby was born on October 14, 1977. She named her Ondrea Jeanette which means 'womanly grace from God'. Kim looked into the beautiful blue eyes of this baby girl. She touched her soft sandy hair. She placed her finger in the palm of her hands with beautiful long fingers. As she held her and gazed into her eyes, she knew this would be another brief moment frozen in time she would not forget. She also knew she had to press on with her life. She signed away her rights. At that moment she knew she would not know where she went or with who.

She felt the love that a mother does after giving birth, but she knew her seventeen year old self was much too ill prepared to be the mother this young life deserved. She wanted the best for this baby. Kim lived at the Sellers home for unwed mothers before the baby arrived. It was a Baptist service agency. They had a nursery at the home. The baby and she came back to the home and Kim left the home when the baby was four days old. Ten days later the baby was put up for adoption at two weeks old. The adoption records were sealed. That day was hard. Her heart was heavy. She must have cried. But still she knew it was right. She had to be honest with herself and make the right choice.

2. AUTO REPAIR

*The sun which passeth through pollutions and itself
remains as pure as before*
    -Book ii, Sir Francis Bacon

*Drink to me only with thine eyes, And I will pledge with
mine. Or leave a kiss but in the cup, And I'll not look
for wine.*

-Ben Johnson, The Forest to Celia

And so each Sunday, Kim went to commune with God in her special way. She went to church. Kim struggled with her loneliness. She got married and then divorced. Nothing seemed to be going right for her. Nevertheless she continued her walk with God in loving worship. Finally Kim allowed that empty feeling in her life. She gave it to God. That sacred space filled her life with possibility. Somehow she still knew through God she was not alone in her circumstances. She let the flow of her life move as if in a stream. She went to college for a while studying nursing. She kept walking her walk with God and some of her pain was being healed. She was going to school and driving her car around town.

Everything was humming along with her life when there was a clinking clanking sound coming from the right front side of the car under the hood. She drove all around town to get that stupid car fixed. Nobody seemed to have any answers for her. She felt this stream was taking her over some rocks now and then. This was one of those days and it frustrated her to no end. Just when she was at the end of her tether she found a mechanic that could in truth fix it. It was as if God had made space to clear a path for her to move in that stream where she needed to go.

Danny was working under a red Chevy Impala aligning the front end when he heard a car drive up to the garage early one morning. There was a clinking clanking sound when the car pulled into a parking space by the office and the engine went off. Next he heard a little tap at the side door. It was early and he thought he would have some quiet time to work on this car before it got too busy in the shop. Perhaps if he ignored it, it would go away. The sound was too persistent. He felt he would never get this car finished until he attended to this customer. Life was humming along for him too. He had won his battle with alcohol and drugs. His first wife and he were partiers and too young to be married. His second wife and he were not compatible. He knew he had made bad choices and was wiser for all of the experience he had. He was ready to move on and enjoy life more fully now. He had set boundaries in his life and was separated from his soon to be ex-wife. He was just getting on his feet after pulling himself away from the negative surroundings that had created the battle he had fought with substances. He and his ex-wife had a daughter together. The ex-wife tried everything she could to keep him from his child. This was painful to him as he wanted to be a father. He wanted to be a hands on type of father who was involved with his child doing what dads do. She kept a wall between his daughter and him. The ex-wife eventually married again and his daughter Tiphanie would bond with her new stepfather. Danny was sad that he was not given the opportunity to be that fatherly presence in her life, but he was glad she had a dad to look up to. That chapter of his life was over and he was just getting settled into his life's routine. He had a deadline for this Impala and was working hard to finish it before the owner arrived. The tapping at the side door would just not go away. Tap Tap Tap.

He pushed himself out from under the car and sprang up to head to the office. He came out of the office door and saw a cute strawberry blond lady with short feathered back hair still tapping at the side door. "May I help you?" She jumped up as if startled and turned around. She was in a hurry and needed her car fixed so she could get to and from school. She cleared her throat and then piped in "Are you Danny Ledford?" "Yes!" "They tell me they can't fix my car over at Liners, but they think you can."

He tried to keep a professional stance. He tried to seem laissez faire, but inside he melted that first moment she looked into his eyes.

She was in such a rush. There were three weeks until finals and she needed to be absolutely sure she wouldn't be a woman alone on a dark street with car trouble when she came home from her night classes. There was no time to chat or worry about other things. She had a tight schedule and it was filled.

She looked at the man and explained the clinking clanking sound. She told him how she kept hearing it. He asked if it still did that when it was idling. She said yes. She told him again about how the Liners people couldn't fix it and how she positively needed this done. She even batted her eyelashes a couple of times hoping that this might get him to squeeze her car into his busy schedule, because his talents were on high demand. Then somewhere between his answering the phone and her batting her eyelashes, both of their eyes met. A spark seemed to fly in and out of their gaze. It was a flash of an instant, but it woke them both up out of their busy lives. A new path was cleared. That path led them to the altar.

3 A SACRED UNION

"Could we forbear dispute and practice love, We should agree as angels do above."

Edmund Waller, *Divine Love*

That first spark lit a flame that joined two souls. That flame engulfed their souls with love and never stopped burning. Years and many car repairs later two pairs of feet side by side walked to that sacred space once more. Lips spoke of having, holding, loving through richer, or poorer, in sickness, and in health, unto death do ye part.

They kissed and joined in a bond that would be in their lives henceforth.

They invited the Lord into their marriage too and He was there. Kim helped Danny realize that he was more than the choices he had made. Through Christ he discovered that he was more than the sum of his past mistakes. The road he had traveled to find Kim was a long one. It was meant to be and they were in love. They both had problems in their past they had created. In their walk with God they both knew they were more than the problems they created.

Kim introduced Danny to church. He felt very close to God. Through going to church he felt he had been remade. A month after they were married, Danny asked the Lord Jesus to come into his heart, and he was baptized by the Holy Spirit. He truly had been given a new life.

Every Sunday Danny and Kim would take time to remember that promise. The water of the Holy Spirit nourished their spirits and their hearts together. They prayed together and worshiped together. Their bond grew like two plants rising up a trellis that were entwined together. Their hopes and dreams were like buds on the vines that were ready to flower.

They were truly in love and felt a loving bond from the first day they met. They had both thought they had gotten through all their time of mourning. He had his work, being a self-employed auto mechanic. He had a life before he met Kim, but felt that the story of his life began when he met her. He knew that when Kim was seventeen she got pregnant and decided to give her baby up for adoption. He could not judge her for this. He knew that he would never be in her shoes to know what it was like to have to make this kind of decision.

They got married and knew they both wanted children and were ready to have one in their lives. She was the woman he wanted to be the mother of his children. He was the man she wanted to be father of her children. Danny had overcome an unsuccessful marriage and had been victorious in his combat with alcohol. Kim had overcome a failed marriage and the loss of her father. They both looked back on it all with wonder. In retrospect they knew it was a miraculously designed process that made them who they were. It made them better people.

They were assured by God's love. They had a feeling that God had brought them together. And often remembered the verse:

*11 For I know the plans I have for you," declares
the LORD, "plans to prosper you and not to harm you,
plans to give you hope and a future.*

- Jeremiah 29:11

Their emotional scars had healed and they
were stronger for it. Of course they knew that grief
is tricky. They knew that sometimes you think it is
all gone and then something happens that can
trigger a memory. When they took this step of
getting married they were risking that once again,
their grief would be exposed. It is a very
complicated and personal thing. But they were
there for each other to carry on to move forward
with their lives and they did. They made plans for
their life together. They shared many joys and had
a rhythm and were well suited to one another
because they loved each other so very much. They
were ready for anything.

4 GIVING A LOSS TO GOD

Illumine, what is low. Raise and support that to the height of this great argument. I may assert eternal providence and justify the ways of God to men.'

-John Milton

Kim and Danny tried to get pregnant for two years to no avail. By July of 1985 they knew they did not want to wait any longer. So they went to the doctor in Chattanooga to find out why they were having difficulty conceiving a baby. Danny had a daughter by a previous marriage but wanted to have a child with Kim. He wanted to have a family with her and was willing to try what was needed to make this happen. A doctor told her there was a new surgery out there that could help her.

They scheduled the surgery at the hospital in Chattanooga. She did all the preparatory blood work and paperwork in the weeks that led up to the surgery. Kim reorganized her work schedule and she made meals in advance. She planned for her mother to come by afterwards and check on her. Danny was involved in all the preparations and appointments. He wanted to make sure everything went smoothly. They were both confident in the cool air-conditioned offices they submitted paperwork to and doctor consultations. Everything was so exacting, clean, and collected in the hospital. They believed nothing could go wrong. Danny held her hand as she went under anesthetic to begin what was supposed to be a simple procedure. They lovingly looked into each other's eyes as she was wheeled away to the operating room. They put all the trust in the doctors belief that everything would come out well. The news they read with their morning coffee was a comfort. They felt confident. On July 13, 1985, Reagan underwent a surgery to remove polyps from his colon. He went under anesthesia and revived a few hours later ready to run our country. All had worked out fine with his operation. She was sure she would come out of her surgery ready to start a family.

She could hear muffled sounds around her like cotton in her ears as she awoke. Everything seemed unreal. She could still taste the anesthesia in her mouth. Her mouth felt hollow and dry. Her heart felt hollow for a reason she did not know yet. She knew something was wrong. Kim's little feet poked out from the blanket. She was still hooked up to IV fluids. She looked so vulnerable and Danny's heart reached out to her. He sat next to her for a while and held her hand. He needed to have a moment with her before he told her. It pained him so much to tell her what had happened.

Her tubes were completely blocked. It was supposed to be a six hour surgery. The doctor came out after forty-five minutes and said that he had given her a complete hysterectomy. He said, if he hadn't, she would have died in six months. Danny woke her up to tell her that they would never have children of their own. He held her hand and looked into her eyes ever so faithfully. She knew, as always, his loyal love would not leave her alone through all of this.

"You had to undergo a complete hysterectomy to save your life. I'm sorry honey," her husband said. Those words fell around her like hollow cardboard boxes dropping on muffled carpet. Waking up to that did not come easy. She was devastated at the thought she and her husband would never have a child to be able to love and call their own. She cried.

It was July in Tennessee. This means hot and rainy. The hot sun beat down on the kudzu. The air was humid and felt too close for comfort. But in the hospital the air was clean and fresh feeling spacious and empty. That sanitary bleachy shiny feeling that echoes in the halls of most hospitals seemed to reflect a hard truth back at Danny as the sun beamed in through the windows. This was the hard truth that they were never going to have a biological child of their own. The doctor had encouraged them to try for this dream of producing a child of their own. Now they realized they were lucky to just have each other. This procedure that could make a path clear for Kim to carry a child of their own was now a false hope. They had a plan and dream that was a second chance, but the path to motherhood and fatherhood that they had chosen was not theirs to choose.

She prayed to God for an answer. Love took her words and remembered them. God heard her prayer that she could have a baby. It is the only thing she was sure of. She wanted to be a mother. She knew she would love to see her child grow, to nurture a new life and be a mother. After a week or two of healing when she was able to think to pray, she looked up to the heavens and prayed to God. God took the words that she spoke and put her in a place that gave her a new life. The love of God took them over and kept her and Danny safe in each other's hearts and in God's hands. There never was an ending to the bond she felt with her husband in the hospital that day. She knew love would have to take her over, because she felt like she could not go forward without it.

She was devastated. Kim was angry with God. She thought she had given another family a chance to have a baby and be a family. She had given them a child and now she was never going to have an opportunity to have a baby to raise herself. She was so very sad, but still they went back to church a month after the surgery. She was still faithful in her walk with God and kept going to church. They were going to Cleveland Christian Church at that time. Pastor Brad Bennett preached God's word. She listened. She was embraced by the community and tried to feel God's love as the choir sang. Her eyes drifted out the window through the pink and purple stained glass windows, and down at the blue carpet, anywhere but up at the cross that first

Sunday back. Finally she allowed herself to realize that the spirit of God was in this place for her healing.

It's hard to be steadfast in our walk with God. Where did we get the idea that things would go according to our own plan? The birds could be singing and the flowers blooming but that does not matter when our plans have been crushed. It is so easy for others to say, "Don't worry, God has a plan for you. This is all in God's hands." She only wished she could take her future into her own hands like the new movie that had just come out "Back to the Future." Unfortunately there was no Delorian time machine to zip into her life and change her fate.

She and Danny were left to wrestle with God over their plans, hopes, and dreams. Their first response could have been "How could you do this to us, God? You ruined our lives. You don't care about us at all."

Their story changed from mournful to miraculous when they turned to God and baseball to ease the pain they felt when they could not have a child of their own. Pete Rose became the all-time hit leader in Major League Baseball, with his 4,192nd hit at the Riverfront Stadium in Cincinnati. This was insult to injury because they were Atlanta

Braves fans. The 1985 season failed to qualify the Braves for the postseason for the third consecutive season, partly due to how well Pete Rose hit the ball. But, they watched baseball on television together anyway, and had something else to set their minds upon.

The hand of God moved in Kim's life. A month later at church, a friend, Sharon Emmerson told Kim about a young woman who was pregnant and might be needing an adoptive placement in a Christian home for her baby. When Sharon told her that she knew a woman with a daughter who was pregnant she was surprised. This young lady was attending church and was now seventeen years old. Now that she had found the Lord, she knew what she had to do. She was pregnant and did not want to abort her baby. She could not care for him and did the right thing to bring this new life into the world. She gave him up knowing it was best for him. Sharon asked Kim and Danny if they wanted the baby and they said "of course we do." They got an attorney and drew up the paperwork. God heard the prayer that Kim was praying. Love filled up all of her empty spaces. Love took her over. Kim recalled the time when she was in the same situation years ago and what a tough decision she had to make concerning her own unborn child. It was the toughest decision in her life. A new awakening opened her heart once again. She thought back to what she had been through to be at this place in her life.

Now the tables had turned completely. She was the receiver this time. She knew the Lord had put Dustin into her life for a reason. She knew it was a special reason from the day she first gazed into his eyes.

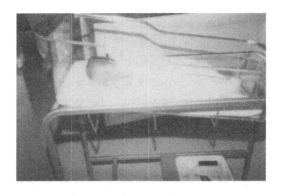

God did care. He brought them Dustin. Did Kim recognize the first moment he came to be? The hospital called Kim and Danny on October 14, 1985 to tell them Dustin's biological mother was in labor. They came to the hospital for his birth. It was eight years to the day from the day her little baby girl was born. It was truly a miracle, maybe even a message from God that through him, with faith, all things are possible. Her Dustin was born at 6:00 a.m. on the fifteenth of October, 1985. That day the Nobel Prize for Economics was awarded to Franco Modigliani. That day Shelley Taylor of Australia made her fastest swim ever around Manhattan Island, in 6 hours, 12 minutes, 29 seconds. That day the Shuttle Columbia carried Spacelab into orbit. But it was far more than that simple time or day or date for Kim and Danny.

It was as if the heavens opened up and placed

Dustin in Kim's arms. It was even more miraculous than a biological birth. An adoptive mother knows and appreciates a new life even more, because she knows it was God's hand who placed her child in her arms. To her, he was the first of his kind. Never before had such a child as this been born. Each baby born is so different and a miracle in the universe worthy of love and awe. That first sound Dustin made touched their hearts. Kim thought he was the ugliest baby she had ever seen. When Danny looked at him for the first time, his heart swelled with pride that he had a son! He knew he would have a little boy to go fishing with and play ball with and do all the things that dads and boys do together.

Dustin's biological mother could not care for him, just as Kim could not care for her daughter. Kim understood the grace and love that must have come from her womb. The church had held this woman in prayer who recognized her ability to carry that baby full term to grace the earth. She gave this little baby his life. She remembered the pain so deep that she herself must have had when she saw the new life that she brought into this world. A part of the biological mother's heart must be closed to let that baby go, when all she wanted was to hold him in her arms. It was once again a moment of majesty when grace was ushered in and mercy took its rightful place in the heart of Dustin's biological mother. She gave Dustin to Kim, who took this new life into her arms, and gazed into his brown eyes. She put her finger in the palm of his tiny little hand. She nestled his soft little head under her chin. It was as if God looked at Dustin's life and decided. The Holy Spirit moved in her life when God wiped her tears of sadness and turned them into joy.

When Dustin first came into the world, he was welcomed with all the loving dreams and attention of any royalty. Whether the pregnancy was difficult, the delivery complex, or the plans for the baby's life unknown, still out came a beautiful baby. There was a moment when Kim forgot that fear of something going wrong in the birthing process as complicated as it was. The anticipation of this baby brought forth joy as she and Danny thought on their drive to the hospital whether he would have open eyes or would be looking around, or would he even have his eyes closed. Dustin was born as an individual that was unique. His existence transcended all the circumstances from which he was created and brought into the world through. It is was if he was placed in Danny and Kim's arms by a power greater than theirs with a connection to heaven, because that is where Dustin came from.

Kim and Danny heard this baby cry and they thought to themselves, "What a wonderful world," just like that Ray Charles song. When they held that child they felt the miracle of life. That is the credit that should be given to every baby born, and Kim and Danny gave this baby this credit and their futures. They felt something stir in their hearts like never before.

The moment they first held Dustin they knew in their hearts this child was theirs, at least for that moment. They knew they looked into the eyes of a future important person. The impermanence of life struck them then. At any moment the birth mother could change her mind, but they felt that parental bond right away. This made them forget about marathon swims, Nobel prizes being won, shuttles being sent out to space, the sadness of Kim's hysterectomy, and the regret of never being a biological parent. When they saw that miracle of life right in front of them, their hearts swelled.

On Oct. 17, 1985, the Ledfords brought home their beautiful baby boy from the hospital. They named him Dustin (valiant) Nathanael (gift of God). Kim's sister, Sherry, cross-stitched this saying as a baby gift in a little frame for Kim and Danny and Dustin.

Not flesh of my flesh
Nor bone of my bone,
But still miraculously my own.

Never forget for a single minute,
You didn't grow under my heart,
But in it.

- Unknown

Kim and Danny knew the Lord had put Dustin into their lives for a special reason from the day they first gazed into his eyes. Raising this child illuminated their ordinary lives. Everyday triumphs became miracles. Minute happenings became acts of God. Their eyes were opened, and all their relations became little blessings and miracles. Thus were the miracles of raising their son. When they adopted this child they had a sense of life's impermanence. They knew that this gift of life for which they were responsible, was so very precious. They knew God put that little one in their arms to care for because life truly was a miracle.

Adjusting to parenthood moved them to a heightened experience of life. The exhaustion of changing diapers, feeding schedules, endless cleaning and hand washing, burping, holding, and loving kept them in a permanent state of awareness.

One night they decided to go out to eat at a steakhouse. It was a huge break from their new routines. They felt like royalty when they went out to eat at a Western Sizzlin Steakhouse. The pride in their parenthood sparkled in their eyes. When the waitress looked at them with interest and asked "how old is he?", They replied "two weeks old." The waitress then remarked, "You're that skinny and you're up and walking?" They just smiled at one another with love in their eyes and said "Yes."

I may not have given you the gift of life but in my heart I know.

The love I feel is deep and real as if it had been so.

For us to have each other is like a dream come true.

No, I didn't give you the gift of life… Life gave me the gift of you.

- Author Unknown

The yearning, and the disappointments, and the waiting were no longer in their hearts. They were parents right then. They were living in the here and now and they were parents and loving it. The official title of 'parent' could be removed by the courts for up to ninety days if contested. They knew this in their minds, but in their hearts, they knew they were the only parents that child ever knew, even if the ninety days were still not up.

When that waitress had asked "Are you sure you are up to being out after giving birth? You look so good," they did not begin to explain the painful path to parenthood they had taken. Their birthing pains were emotional, not physical. They knew they wanted this child and they were sure. They were ready to face the world as parents. Their hearts glowed with parenthood. Another time a woman at Walmart peered into the car seat and said "You sure can tell who his daddy is." They chuckled and went on with their lives as if Dustin was theirs from conception. No child could have fit into their lives any better than Dustin fit into theirs. Dustin walked like Danny and looked like him, too.

The world gathered around this precious new life. The once romantic, love-struck married couple became doting parents. A close bond formed from the hours of holding him with his little head nestled against their chests. Those still, quiet moments when he suckled milk warmed

Kim's and Danny's hearts. Danny sweetly hummed a song that sounded as if it were borrowed from the angels in heaven. Dustin became the center of their lives.

Dustin made each day new to them. Every little breath, coo, gurgle, and movement was to them a miracle sent by God. They were now the family they wanted to be. That spark when Kim's and Danny's eyes first met was now realized in Dustin, through their prayers and petitions to God.

Here was this new soul, purely their responsibility. He was the kind of baby that had a clear, commanding cry. He was a soul with the love of life ready to be conquered. He was a baby that wanted to go, go, go. Kim and Danny took him there, and as a family their adventures exploded!

Their biggest fear was that his birth mother was going to come and take him. She had ninety days from the day he was born to change her mind. During those ninety days Kim lived in constant fear and a heightened awareness of the real treasure of life that Dustin was. When Dustin was a month old he was in the hospital with an unexplained fever for five days. Nurses gave him shots in his little legs. Kim was mostly awake for four days and nights just holding him, because that was the only thing that kept him quiet. After four days Danny made her go out for a while.

Kim went to a store, Parks Belk, (now Belks) and bought a little pair of tennis shoes, a little rattle, and the bumper pad for his crib. She remembered saving the receipt because she was so terrified that the birth mother was going to change her mind and come and take him back. Now she was terrified that she could lose him from this fever, as well.

Family and friends were supportive. Kim's mother had just come back from Hawaii and brought Dustin a red baseball cap that said "Little Slugger" on it, knowing how much they watched baseball together. Grandma had an inkling that this baby's new daddy would be one day practicing ball in the back yard with that little tyke. It was an awakening in her soul. She knew he was a weak child who needed special care because the doctors were telling them that he had a special blood condition that weakened him called Hypo-Gama Globulin Anemia. Grandma realized that every minute they had with Dustin was special. Dustin infused a new light into their family that shined on everyone and reminded each one of them that that none of us on this earth can be owned by another.

They put his healing in God's hands and gave him the medicine that was prescribed and he thrived. He was a reminder that we are all living on borrowed time. Each life is sacred and our fate is in God's hands. Once Dustin was better and home from the hospital, Kim had time to catch up on sleep, drink her morning coffee, and read the daily paper. One quiet morning she saw a poem that struck her heart. She clipped it out and tucked it away in her memory box to remind her how blessed she was. The poem was entitled <u>A Child Of Mine</u>, by Edgar Guest. It started out saying….

"I will lend you, for a little time,
A child of mine, ……" She read it and thought it spoke to her condition. She cut it out carefully and put it in her memorabilia box to reflect upon someday.

Three weeks after Dustin's birth things were becoming a routine. They were a family. Kim and Danny decided it was time to have a baby dedication, a public commitment before God, their family, and their church. This dedication allowed them to express publicly their desire to lead and spiritually nurture Dustin to love God and others.

It was a beautiful day. The air was crisp. The

leaves were changing to their bright orange and reds. The whole world seemed like a gigantic Renoir painting. Kim's mother came to church prepared in her thoughtful way with a dedication poem she had written on the day Dustin was born. That third day of November in 1985 Kim read it aloud to all.

Oh Father , what an awesome gift You've given us.
A miracle, a little son so precious.
A life within our hands to hold. To love to cherish
and yes, to mold.

And father we thank you for the love You've shown.
By giving us Your son Your very own.
To die for us so that we might live.
And to enjoy the blessing You so freely give.
So father as we give our son back to you.
With hearts full of love and thanksgiving too.
We pray we will be what you want us to be.
And be Your example for our son to see.
Yes Father and at this moment of his dedication with
a prayer of thanksgiving and supplication we
gratefully praise you with hearts so thankful and ask
You to bless our little Dustin Nathanael.

So even before they were absolutely sure of being Dustin's forever family, they dedicated him to God. They knew what kind of parents they wanted to be. They prayed they would be the best parents

Dustin could ever have.

Kim and Danny planned to always be honest with Dustin and keep lines of communication open. They did not want to be the kind of parents that would tell their kids things like: "When the ice cream truck plays music, it means they're out of ice cream." or "There is a little man who lives in the fridge that turns the light on for you." They set out to selflessly let Dustin find his way in life and encourage him and empower him. If their story unfolded the way they hoped it would, he would grew to be a well-adjusted young man. They would be very conscientious and kind. They would listen to Dustin and take his views into account. Dustin in turn would listen to them and trust them.

Dustin's sleep routine was complicated. Most people need time to wind down before bed, and babies are no different. Kim and Danny had a bedtime routine for Dustin that helped him get relaxed. They would rock him and rock him until they could finally take him and lay him down in the crib. This bedtime routine was an easy strategy as well as bonding. Some nights Dustin would be all out of sorts and no rocking would seem to do the trick. So, Kim and Danny would drive around for hours to get Dustin to go to sleep.

They tried so many strategies to get him to sleep. They soon realized it was important to answer the biggest question. How could they get Dustin to nap and to slow down once in a while? They soon deduced he was a child of motion. He was always on the go. He was the kind of baby that people observe for long periods of time and then wonder "Does he have an off button?" Kim and Danny had fantastic insights about his baby sleep.

Kim and Danny were told so many things that they were "supposed to" do with a baby. When they went out in public, they got advice from passersby. Older folks told them one thing. Younger folks told them another. They realized that very few babies die from all these different strategies, but still they wanted to do what was right and sometimes it left them feeling perplexed. When they asked questions about swaddling, pacifiers, baby swings, the eat-play-sleep methods, and other things, they got widely different answers depending on whom they asked.

They wondered if baby swings were safe. They knew that Dustin would fall asleep in the car. They knew that when they rocked him, he might fall asleep. Other times they tried the baby swing to get him to sleep, and it worked.

Their pediatrician told them that about 85% of babies can go right to sleep in their cribs But, still there is that 15% that needs to constantly be moving. That was Dustin. In his case a baby swing was a godsend. When Kim needed to do laundry, and Dustin was fussing, the swing calmed him down. It worked. She got a moment of peace and quiet and could rest a bit.

When Kim saw Dustin dozing in the swing, she felt it was the perfect time to put him in the crib. After all, the pediatrician said the best place for him to sleep was in the crib, face down. So she tried to slowly turn the swing from high to medium rocking to low. Click, click, click, ker plunk, back and forth slowly it went. She gently, ever so gently, eased her hands down the sides to softly pick him up. He was still asleep. She gently lifted him up into her arms ready to put into the crib, and "WAAAAHHHHH!" This day was not going to be the nap of champions. So back he went in the baby swing, cranking it to low. He was not happy, so she set it to medium, and he fell asleep and she took him out again to try to put him back in the crib.

Some days she was lucky and he would go to sleep right off. Other days he would cry until she put him back in the swing.

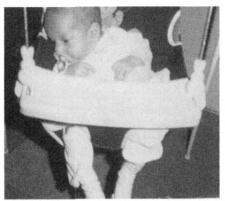

Nevertheless, they were positively grateful for that wonderful baby swing. Eventually, Dustin had adjusted to sleeping in the crib all the time. So you may ask "If your baby falls asleep in the swing, then you take him out to lay him in the crib and he wakes up and starts crying, what are you supposed to do?" Try it again, and again, and again, until you succeed. And that is what Kim and Danny did.

Danny and Dustin at18 months

5 ON YOUR MARK , GET SET, CRAWL, WALK, RUN!!

"A baby's feet, like seashells pink, Might tempt, should heaven see meet, An angel's lips to kiss, we think, A baby's feet."

-Algernon Charles Swinburne

Kim's friend knitted tiny baby booties which were soon outgrown. Dustin's first pair of shoes were bought in case he would walk soon. Each day was new. Each season cast a new light on the little person that was emerging from this little package that was once a baby.

"Blowing pegs," some people call it. "Cutting teeth" is the more universal expression. However you describe it, the gummy grin that turns into a mouthful of gleaming teeth happens over several years. But when the first tooth peeks through, it is reason to celebrate. When Dustin cut his first tooth he was almost seven months old. It was May 7, 1986. One day Kim was just playing and laughing with Dustin as he was rocking in his swing. Only this time when he smiled, and his seven month old mouth opened as wide and as adorable as it always was, she saw a flash of something white. Back and forth he went, and each time she couldn't believe it. She had to get a closer look but he would rock back on the swing. Finally she saw it. It was a teeny tiny itty bitty little baby tooth poking its way through his gums. Immediately she ran to the phone and called Danny.

The defining moment of toddlerhood for babies is the day they take their first steps. It is such a joy. They learn to walk on their own, and from then on, you are chasing after them and wondering where they are going and what they are into. Sometimes they hold onto your fingers and walk with you a lot. Sometimes they stand and wave their arms around in the air for balance and stand

alone, but their feet stay firmly planted. Sometimes their first steps are more like stomps. They pick up one foot assuredly high and then drop it while trying to catch their balance. Then they try the same thing again with their other foot. It is like watching a Sumo wrestler getting ready to fight. Sometimes they get perplexed and give up for weeks until they try again. Some children are more like bulldozers. Their first steps are more like a fast sprint and they run to their destination point with that determined look in their eyes. Sometimes they fall at their destination, but they pick themselves up, keep going, and never stop running throughout their lives. This was the kind of child Dustin was.

When Dustin was eleven months, old he

learned to walk on the beach. At first they were just playing in the sand, building a huge sand castle. It was time to come in from the hot sun and get some lunch. Kim saw him just standing there playing with the castle. He was eating the sand, like some kids do, so she went to get him, but he didn't want to go. When she went to get him again, he bit her. She retreated long enough to catch her breath, and then with new energy went a final time to grab him, and he just ran away from her. His strides grew and grew. At first he crawled all over the house. Then he climbed. That one day at the beach he walked. After that he tested his land legs for a month and then he was a runner. He loved the open spaces on the beach just like his mom and dad. He liked the space because it felt like he could run forever. They liked it because they could see everywhere he went. He knew even then what he loved to do, and did it.

While on their beach vacation, they went to a store and spent a few minutes in the toy department. On the shelf was a rocking horse. They let Dustin try it, and then put it back on the shelf. When it was time to go, he would have none of that idea, he jumped up and down, he cried, he wailed, he almost swooned. "Reecie reecie reecie...." he repeated over and over again. He was inconsolable. They realized then what "reecie" meant. It meant "horsey." Horsey, was what he was trying to say. Since they still had some vacation money left for emergencies, and in Danny's mind this was an emergency, they bought that rocking horse. Dustin rode that horse day and night from the moment they pulled in the driveway. For years they would look back on that vacation and realize that emergency money they used on that short beach trip was money well spent.

Dustin's first birthday party was amazing. He had his first bite of cake, after a year of baby food and bottles. Along with that first bite of cake come so many other firsts, such as eating with their fingers, turning the pages of a book, or taking first steps. This little person was starting to explore the world and would taste a sour lemon for the first time. That sticky, gleeful, surprised face they make is special. That is why everyone wants to be there at that first birthday party. They had leftover birthday cake all week. Dustin's birthday fell on a Wednesday that year so the party was the following Saturday. It was a wondrous shock to realize that their baby was a year of age! Where did the time go?

The morning of the party, Kim was nervous. She had an assortment of so many emotions that she felt all over the place! Dustin had a "Sesame Street" birthday. He had his own little cake to eat and squish with his own little fingers. There was also a Big Bird and Cookie Monster cake for the friends and family. She was dying to make her son happy. Everyone enjoyed themselves, especially Dustin. Even though he had skipped his nap and was quite tired, he was a genuinely good sport! He was all smiles and giggles until he reached the last stretch of the party. His attention began to lag when he was unwrapping the gifts,. This was okay, since he was only one year old, and didn't grasp the whole concept of a 'birthday party' yet! Dustin was the life of this party. The world was fresh and new to him. He never did stop loving a good party. This day he was spoiled, but to a reasonable extent. They were happy that he received gifts that would be useful. He got a Little Tykes slide that he slid down over and over again. He started getting creative going down the slide on his stomach. Kim said "Don't do that or you will bust your nose." He kept doing it and landed face first on the carpet. He had a little scrape but kept going. He would be the kind of child who learned through experience. He started to run out of steam as the party went on. He cuddled his new little blue teddy bear for a brief moment. He lackadaisically pushed his Little Tykes train that he could ride all by himself. He smiled lightly at the clothes for the upcoming summer, and a floater for the pool. All of these were great things! Eventually he would learn to appreciate each of those nice gifts. But, honestly,

Dustin still loved his rocking horse more than anything. Years after that special day he would jump on that horse and be the little cowboy he was

as a toddler.

They couldn't have asked for a better birthday party for Dustin. Friends and family came together and truly made that day extremely special for Dustin, and for themselves. But what Kim and Danny liked most about the party was that they had each other and that was everything. Those memories were well preserved.

Finally, the day arrived when the ninety days

was over. The adoption could not be called into question in a court of law. But still, the laws were such that they had to wait a year for the proceedings to be complete. It was time for the adoption to be finalized in January of 1987. While those ninety days seemed to last a lifetime, the year following did so as well. The day came to appear in court in front of the Judge. They could now be the parents they had hoped to be forever. Kim and Danny were dressed up and ready to go. Kim was so excited. She wore a red dress with bows and a matching purse. Her mother went with them. Kim went sauntering out of the courthouse with pride and happiness now that she was officially graced with the title of 'Mother'!

Just as she handed Dustin over to her mom, Kim's high heel was wedged in a crack between the loose gravel on the concrete steps. Her ankle and foot were stuck and she turned while her ankle did not. The rest of her tumbled down the steps headfirst and her skirt flew up over her head. She can remember looking up and seeing about seven pairs of wing-tipped shoes which were under fancy suits belonging to the attorneys ready for a day at court. The army of suits and wing-tips ran over to ask if she was all right. Although she was pretty humiliated, she was just glad to know Dustin's adoption was final, and he was theirs to have and to hold, from this day forward. She was one happy mama.

That evening she and Danny held a party at

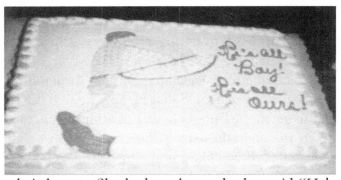

their home. She had a cake made that said "He's all boy and he's all ours." Dustin was cherished. Kim always told him that his birth mother couldn't give him things that she wanted him to have and so she found a family who could. That was the same way she felt about her daughter. When Dustin came out of the delivery room he was an ugly baby, but it didn't take long for him to be the apple of her eye. Kim always told Dustin he wasn't born in her tummy, but in her heart. She could honestly assure him he grew in her heart instantly. Dustin was beloved. He grew into a beautiful toddler with lightning speed. She knew in her heart that God was going to use Dustin in a mighty way, because God chose to let Dustin live. There were people encouraging Dustin's biological mother to have an abortion, but she chose to go through the pregnancy and give him up for adoption. Kim was grateful she had made this choice.

When Dustin was 16 months old, Danny came home from work to discover another surprise. It was as if Dustin was waiting to show him some new action once again. Dustin, being the kinetically charged child that he was, figured out a way to get in the laundry basket and ride all the way down the stairs in it by sliding down at just the right angle. It was like a home-made roller coaster and he loved it. Kim thought it would be o.k. after the first few times, since the stairs were carpeted and it was hard to veer off the track. The "yippee yeah" shrieks of joy and laughter were too adorable to put a stop to all of this fun.

Kim and Dustin came to the door rosy cheeked, aerobically aerated, and ready to show daddy how to have fun with a simple laundry basket. Dustin was especially animated and truly wanted to show off for Daddy. He hooped. He hollered. He raised his little arms in joy shrieking "yippee yeah" one too many times. Finally his enthusiasm knocked him off kilter enough to send him into the bannister. He turned and flipped up in the air and down again. This last time he was not laughing, with his injuries needing stitches.

Dustin spent his nights in a baby crib until he was two. Like many children, change was hard for him. When he was two, Danny had built him a toddler bed. They decided to ease Dustin into the new routine. The first night they put the new bed in his room next to his crib. The second night they put the mattress in the toddler bed. They thought all was well, and they gave him that typical talk. "Now you are a big boy! You get to sleep in a big boy's bed. Look! Daddy made this just for you!" They tucked him in all nice and tight. They kissed his little cheek goodnight. They thought they had triumphed once again. Two hours later they went to check on him. He was laying on the floor under his crib. Their hearts sank. He was still attached to his old bed. This same adjustment between toddlers and their big beds happens everywhere. For every parent a child's struggle with change is new and delicate. Helping Dustin cope with this big new big bed world that laid before him was humbling and kept their hearts real and tender.

Potty training was so hard. Diapers and wipes are easy, but when a parent knows it's time to put those "big boy" pants on, it is a test of wills. Some parents try the natural approach where their children are kept outside and forced to become aware through a series of accidents. Some parents try books, lectures, toys, and playgroups. Most parents feel like they are going to pull their hair out at some point in the process. The grandparents gently remind us that there are almost no adults out there who never were toilet trained. Every parent working on that skill with their child worries if their child will still be wearing diapers to kindergarten. Kim and Danny's patience was tried by this test of wills. They tried rewarding him with candy, they tried stern words. Finally when Kim just told Dustin that she was not going to buy any more diapers, he gave in and used the toilet from then on.

Regular everyday routines set Dustin apart from others, and made him a Ledford. They set them apart from others because they were now the one and only Kim, Danny, and Dustin Ledford family with their own personal family patterns and personality. The choices they made of how to sit, visit, clean, and part their hair were uniquely Kim and Danny's and made their lives rich. They passed these routines down from generation to generation without knowing it. Every morning Danny had the routine of shaving. Just as Danny watched his own father shave, Dustin watched Danny every morning. Every day Kim washed the dishes. Just as Kim watched her mother wash dishes, and Kim's mother watched her mother wash the dishes, so did Dustin watch Kim wash the dishes. This was why Kim learned to wash dishes like her grandmother. These outward routines are passed down from generation to generation through what we say and do around our children. These are the traits that we inherit that mean more to us than we know. These traits run deep into our core and move through our lives in unseen ways. This is uniquely embraced and known by an adopted child because at some point in time they wrestle with the realization that there is a part of them biologically like their birth parents, yet they recognize the exterior influence of their adopted parents that made them who they are. Dustin watched everything his parents did and drank in the Ledford family ways.

Kim and Danny taught Dustin both by example and words. Danny showed his son how the little things in the river's flow of everyday life. Just like the fish that washes up on the shore from the flood that one puts back into the river, It matters. Those seemingly small routines like shaving, kissing your wife goodbye every morning, and keeping your napkin in your lap matter. Does it matter in the grand scheme of things? It matters to that fish in the flood, and it mattered to Dustin who was taken out of one stream and put in the stream of life with his parents.

These everyday habits they shared were important to Dustin, Kim, and Danny, because they built a bridge to live the best life they could. Dads often pass these skills and habits on to their sons such as how to change their own oil, how to ride a bike, how to throw a ball or shoot a basket, how to shine shoes, how to tie a necktie, and how to shave.

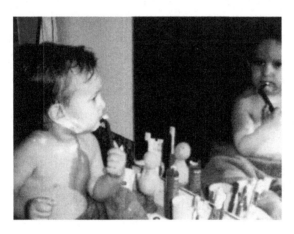

Picture of Dustin Shaving

When Dustin was two, he would sit with Danny in the bathroom and just watch him every morning. Shaving was a true rite of passage for Dustin. He watched his father shave. He watched everything Danny did and imitated him.

One day he grabbed the shaving cream and a razor with his little hands. He liked to pretend to be Daddy. Danny supervised and took out the razor. He hoisted him on top of the counter. He let him feel the foamy cream in-between his little fingers. It was a thrill to him. He liked to look in the mirror and pretend to be grown up. He pretended he was daddy as he looked at himself in the mirror. He made the same movements, expressions, and looked like a miniature Danny. He did not know then that this was a special moment. Mommy did though. She took a picture.

Dustin's learning to shave process took time, too. It seemed as if he was in awe as he watched Danny drag a sharp blade across his face and make the whiskers miraculously disappear! Danny used disposable razors because electric razors bothered his skin. Beside his razor he kept a bladeless plastic razor for Dustin to play with. Danny still has that razor in the top drawer of the guest bathroom. Growing up and learning to shave is an adventure for every boy. Sometimes we have guidance. Sometimes we do not. But rarely do we forget this journey.

Dustin grew up from a little boy in a sailor suit to a man that had whiskers. He was ready to

face the world and grow up to be a man because he had a dad to follow and he took his lead. This tender moment is so rich for many dads and sons. Rites of passage are those moments that come along that deserve a little special attention, a spotlight. So often they get lost in history. Rodney, their barber at R &B Barbershop in Cleveland, Tennessee is willing to wager you that most men you meet will have a story of some kind about the first time they shaved. It often turns out to be a very revealing story about a special someone. That special person for Dustin was his dad. He looked up to him and loved him. This fatherly rite of passage was highlighted, marked, and remembered in his life, but it may be one of the least talked about important events in a man's life. It was a step toward manhood Dustin took.

It is a step every man takes. This picture is a window into the span of time we influence our children.

Every boy is different and develops at a different rate. Dustin might have been 13 or so when hair began to be noticeable. He might have said to his Dad things like, "...the guys are giving me a hard time always asking me if my upper lip is dirty," or "...Mr. Smith down the street says my mustache is coming in great." They all knew then it was time to get out the real razor.

Along with all the family routines of shaving, breakfast, and dressing were the medicines Dustin had to take for his Hypo-Gama Globulin Anemia. Even though he had God to lead the way in his life he still needed a dose of amoxicillin every day because his immune system was unquestionably fragile. The first four years of his life he regularly had a broken bone or stitches. Once he was swinging on the monkey bars and did a flip over the slide and Kim heard a crack. That was the first of many broken bones for Dustin. In fact, Kim would alternate hospitals when she took him in to mend his latest bruise, sprain, or broken bone. She did this for fear of being reported for child abuse. It was almost a family joke. He felt no fear of heights. He loved to climb, and run, and feel the earth beneath his feet. He loved to feel the breeze run through his hair. He loved to splash in water. He loved life. He lived life wide open.

They knew at some point Dustin would outgrow the need for training wheels, but they didn't anticipate it happening so soon. Those training wheels on his bicycle did not last long, however. Dustin was five years old when it was time to graduate to the use of only two wheels. Removing the training wheels from Dustin's bicycle was a rite of passage. All he needed was a push across the front yard once or twice and he was ready to go. The training wheels were a crutch he no longer needed. He was not scared for a moment when they were taken off.

He had great balance. His bicycle was just one more thing that gave him a sense of independence. He could bike to friends' houses in the neighborhood, to the park, and to the library. They used to walk, but biking was so much faster.

There was a different kind of balance Kim and Danny worked to maintain, such as if and when to push more, or how to keep Dustin safe. When Dustin zipped down the road, Kim's heart swelled with pride, but then she worried if she had pushed him too far. Kim thought to herself at night: "I will encourage. I will cajole. I will console. I will doctor the scabs. I will help him balance. I will wipe away his tears. I will help him back on the bike. I will let go. He will balance without me." But in the light of day there was no time for that inner dialogue, for with two minutes of practice, he was off!

Upon reflection, she wondered if the training wheels were, in reality, just for the parents after all. She and Danny were all about finding balance between safety and perseverance, not just on a bike, but in life overall. Dustin quickly found out for himself the balance between being safe and learning to ride on his own. The parental job of nurturing, holding back, then letting go, never stopped.

Life seemed to settle down again once Dustin was in half day Kindergarten. Dustin no longer needed as much attention because of his compromised immune system. He didn't catch as many germs as he used to. Kim thought she had the freedom to be able to go back to work. Kim dropped him off at school and went to work. After half day Kindergarten, Dustin went to Danny's mother's house to play at Grandma's until Kim came to pick him up after work. He was a bundle of energy always actively engaging with his surroundings. He couldn't go outside when he was at Grandma's, so he resorted to recreation inside. A child with that much energy couldn't help but get into things in the house. One fateful day they learned that Dustin needed more supervision than they realized. Dustin knocked over the kerosene heater and flames were everywhere. Dustin, true to his brave-heart nature, refused to leave the house until the Fire Department came and rescued his grandma. He stood at the glass door of the house yelling "Mamaw, Mamaw, get my Mamaw." This incident made them rethink whether or not Kim should go back to work. After this Kim was a stay at home mom.

First grade was a milestone for Dustin. Kim did a lot as a Room Mother. Everything went well in first grade, except that Dustin talked a lot! The teacher had a conference with Kim one day and explained how he was often in trouble for talking too much. The teacher tried everything. He almost got a spanking at home, but Papaw George intervened and said "Nobody's gonna spank my grandson!" Too much talking was the worst

problem they had to deal with. He was so enthusiastic about school, especially on picture day when he would always be well dressed.

Dustin had an independent spirit. One day Kim couldn't find Dustin. They were living at Marquis Apartments, because they were in-between selling their house and buying a new one. Kim checked the next apartment complex where Dustin knew he could play. All the boys and girls were crowded around a dumpster. When Kim arrived, Dustin peaked out from inside a dumpster. He was waist deep in trash and said "Look what I found Mamma!" He had found notepads, paper, and pencils among other things. She took him home and scrubbed him down and was horrified with the thought of all the germs he had been in. But Dustin didn't see it that way, for to him, the dumpster was a magical wonderland of free fun. Living in the apartment complex with dumpsters was only temporary.

They moved into the house where they still live to this day when Dustin was six. It was a nice ranch home on two acres in a distinguished subdivision. Kim loved the two baths, the double garage, and the nice neighbors. It was even close to the golf course. Dustin no longer went dumpster diving in the new subdivision. New things to explore were always on Dustin's horizon.

Danny and Dustin built a tree house to help channel Dustin's creativity at the old house. They spent three or four weeks building this tree house, putting it between the two trees where they lived. When they eventually sold that house and were ready to move, Dustin said "Daddy but what are we going to do about my tree house?" So Danny had the tree house moved from the old house to the new one, just for Dustin. Danny had to get a wrecker to come to the old house to remove Dustin's tree house. Then the wrecker had to drive across town with it to the new house they had just moved to. It didn't matter what they were doing, they did it for Dustin. Nothing else seemed to matter that much.

Dustin was always one step ahead of everything, just like the day he lost his first baby tooth. He felt that funny wiggly feeling from the tooth. Danny and Kim were wishing he would just pull it out all on his own, but it dangled there for days. They feared that it might get infected, or that the way Dustin played with it might be a distraction to the other children at school. Dustin knew that the Tooth Fairy was going to come and leave money under his pillow and he was looking forward to cashing in on the tooth. He just didn't think that a few coins would be worth pulling out a piece of himself. Days passed. The day finally came when Kim and Danny told him they were going to pull it out. They tried to convince him it wouldn't hurt that much. Dustin began to scream. Danny sat him on the bathroom vanity, while Dustin continued screaming. Finally they just reached in his mouth and pulled it out. It came out in a flash.

In some cultures that tooth would be replaced with a small gift from a mouse. Other families would throw their child's baby teeth in an ocean or a field, at the sun, or on the roof. In some places baby teeth are thrown on the roof or under the house, depending on whether they want the new tooth to grow up or down. All of these traditions serve to downplay the blood and loss of the tooth. Childhood for Dustin was magical and he believed in the Tooth Fairy. Dustin believed that anything was possible. This magical stage was enchanting and fun. Dustin had faith in all the wonder life had to offer.

Understanding the workings of the Tooth Fairy was a complex job to seven-year-old Dustin. He tried to figure the whole thing out on his own, as always. His pediatric dentist explained that the Tooth Fairy took all her tooth loot to her magic castle. Later on Dustin was able to pick up on clues. He noticed interesting differences in the amounts of money and gifts his friends received in exchange for discarded teeth. (This could be explained by the high cost of dental work, and quality of her find.) He looked and he watched and one day he understood the 'magic' of money miraculously appearing for his tooth. It helped ease the pain and worry of losing a tooth. He always understood the magic of life. He knew the magic of losing a tooth was not always fun, and neither was the magic of life. It was the magic, or grand appreciation of the little things however, that made life magical.

Birthdays, vacations, Christmas, Halloween, Easter, Mother's Day, Father's Day, and Fourth of July were joyous times for Dustin. He embraced Goofy on their first trip to Disney World.

Here he is ready to go down the tracks.

He went to the Cleveland Speedway, and took a

tour of the famous Daytona Speedway. The speedway was an adventure he tore into with glee. His eyes would light up at these special moments just like they did when Santa came. Dustin had a great imagination and saw himself as a caped crusader ready for duty at the first sign of the bat light! He imagined himself striking fear into the hearts of the unjust! He pretended to scare criminals. He was a cute little dark knight fearlessly protecting the neighborhood. His parents were still near as they went trick-or-treating. He pretended to take down his dad with his immense strength in this disguise which ended up in a tickling match. Kim sewed him the best costume ever. This Batman jumpsuit with attached boot tops and arm gauntlets, utility belt, courageous cape and masked headpiece (to hide his secret identity) was the most fun costume ever! In Dustin's mind's eye Cleveland Tennessee was now safe for all trick-or-treaters.

Every day was exciting with Dustin. When he was about five years old, Ninja Turtles had become popular. One day after watching the Teenage Mutant Ninja Turtles movie, an eerie quiet settled in the house. It was that kind of worrisome quiet only a mother senses and feels, and it led Kim to run outside and look up.

When she popped her head out of the front door, she saw him on his "cozy coupe," (an orange car with a yellow roof that looks like a Volkswagen.) He loved that toy. Most kids ride in their cozy coupes. Dustin was riding on top of his. Dustin was going down the driveway yelling "Cowa Bunga Dude." He was picking up speed on the incline in the driveway, and steering was not an option. He landed on a tree, fell off of the car, and broke his ankle. Once again Kim was in the Emergency Room with Dustin and his Ninja Turtle "Cowabunga" plans that had gone awry. By age six, he had experienced two broken bones.

Christmas was a special time for Dustin every

year. All of Kim's sisters who were able, would gather at Kim's mother's house on Christmas Eve. Aunt Sherry would always bring homemade beef jerky. Aunt Sherry and Uncle Gene didn't always have a lot of money, but their simple gift was always Dustin's favorite. It was their love and warmth that infused the flavor of that jerky. This was the best Christmas gift that had the love behind it, just like the love of God that gave us Jesus. Santa never forgot Dustin. He was a good boy. The family enjoyed a nice dinner and celebrated the joys of the season.

Dustin played on the stairs with all the old toys that Grandma saved from when her children were young. Dustin was entranced by the unusual toys and could play for hours with them. This night was even better because he played with his cousins, too.

That was the year Dustin's interest was captured by the Ghost Busters toys Santa gave him. So Kim and Danny, who were preparing the presents and toys, snuck away from Grandma's house while Dustin was playing. Sometimes little ones need more proof that Santa is real. They went into their house and got some boots out and put soot on them. Then they made tracks through the house as if Santa had walked across the floor. The false evidence looked so real. They were proud of themselves. That evening when they came home, they let Dustin go into the house first. He went to check to see if Santa had come yet. He came running back. "Mommy, Daddy, Mommy, Daddy, Santa IS REAL!!!!! Look! Look! I told you so!!"

Growing up, Dustin was the happiest child. He made you laugh, cheered you up and made many friends. Every step he took showed the world a certain sign of grace. Kim knew there was a special purpose in his life. He was everything that was bright and clean. His little hands playing in the sand spilled joy all over the space around him. He could fly like the wind on his bike and still come back around for a kiss. It seemed impossible that this Glory of God would greet his parents each day with a kiss for Mommy and Daddy. They held him and rocked him when he woke up with bad dreams. They felt the arms of God holding them when he rested on their shoulders. That magic time when their child slept in their arms was like no other. The innocence and light of God showed through Dustin's face.

When Dustin was eight years old Danny and Kim bought him his first motorcycle. As soon as Dustin got his motorbike he gave his mom a ride. He took off and they nearly ran into the van. She put her leg out to prevent him from crashing, but in the process she got a big welt on her thigh from being burned by the tailpipe when she fell off the back. He said, "Mama I am so sorry, but I just didn't have any control of this thing because there was so much weight on the back." That hurt more than the burn on the back of her leg!

Dustin had plenty of places to go in Cleveland, Tennessee all of his years growing up. It was a good place to raise a child. He passed his first driver's license test at the Department of Motor Vehicles right there in the north end of Bradley County. He shopped in downtown Cleveland at Flowers 'n Things Florist on Mouse Creek Road to buy a corsage for his date for the dance. He passed by the Fireworks Plus, Exit 20 and Cleveland Toyota just 15 minutes north from Hamilton Place Mall in Chattanooga to buy a round of fireworks to surprise his friends or family.

Dustin was part of a town that still had that old town feeling. Store-fronts in the town center are lined with tall lampposts that shine at night and have decorative flags on them celebrating each holiday. He stood on the side of the road to watch the Christmas parade that was a big deal in town. Dustin was always in awe of the floats promoting the local businesses going down Broad Street. He stood among the Halloween crowds that attracted thousands of people to Broad Street. As he got older he bought apple fritters with his mom and dad on their way to a baseball game at the Cleveland Apple festival. They liked visiting the Cleveland Apple Festival where the children's area was free.

They were happy to be in this town with Dustin, for it was a town that celebrated children, just as Kim and Danny celebrated their child. Dustin felt safe growing up here. He was safely nestled between a series of low hills and ridges almost fifteen miles west of the Blue Ridge Mountains. Sometimes he and Grandpa liked to venture east about fifteen miles to fish. They ran into the Chickamauga Lake impoundment of the Tennessee River. Other times they went for river trout, north of Cleveland to the Hiwassee River which provided water that is fed from mountain streams and spring snow melting. There was a lot of rain in Cleveland with all those rivers moving water around them and the mountains encircling the town. This made water sports a must for Dustin.

Rain boots, rain coat, and an umbrella were a regular part of their lives. Dustin loved to splash around in puddles and was happy he could usually count four to five inches of rain every month. Houses were being built up and Dustin made friends with all the new youngsters moving in. The town continued to grow to 41,000 people by 2010. Industry categorically did well in Cleveland with friendly people who had a strong work ethic. Whirlpool Corporation, Amazon.com, Coca-Cola Refreshments, Mars, Inc., Duracell, Bowater, and Olin Corporation, among others, provided good jobs for people. There were many people adding their own specialness to Cleveland as the years went on. None could compare with the way Dustin chose to live his life wide open.

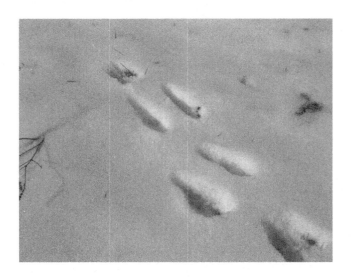

6 RABBIT TRACKS IN THE SNOW

"You hear that boy laughing? You think he's all fun;
But the angels laugh, too, at the good he has done. The
children laugh loud as they troop to his call, And the poor
man that knows him laughs loudest of all."

-Oliver Wendell Holmes

From those first steps on the beach there were
now three sets of footprints walking together --
Kim and Danny walking side by side and Dustin's

93

far ahead.

Those little feet tracked rabbits in the snow, ran many home runs on baseball fields, pressed hard on bicycle pedals, jumped, climbed and stomped occasionally. They were always on the move, and most of all, they were fearless and fun.

Danny and Kim would stop in their tracks and look at each other in the same way they did the first time their eyes met. They knew this was God's plan for them to be parents together. The joy of parenthood colored their lives through its ups and downs. They could see things through the eyes of a child in all its heartfelt innocence. Every hour of light and dark was a miracle to them and every cubic inch of space led them to more new miracles to explore.

As the seasons changed, so did Dustin. He grew more intent on embracing life and doing as much as he could every minute of every day. He had more and more ideas about where to go, what to do, and he knew why he wanted to do these things. Kim and Danny were right beside or closely trailing behind every step Dustin took. They were present in his life enjoying the rich process of parenthood unfold as they watched their son develop in sports, play, and adventures on the way to becoming his own person. Sometimes grandpa and grandma ('Papaw and Mamaw') would tag along, too. Autumn passed and winter snow fell one year, which was rare. Dustin tracked rabbits, hunted squirrels, and fished.

This quiet time in the winter snow was a rich time. The moonlight hitting the white snow was poetic. So often we miss the poetry of life that only catches our attention in retrospect. Thomas Buchannan Read's poem, "Drifting," captures this moment.

"Yon deep park goes. Where Traffic blows. From lands of sun to lands of snows; -- Yon happier one, Its course is run. From lands of snow to lands of sun."
-- Thomas Buchanan

Papaw and Dustin ran through the deep parts of the woods. They traced rabbit tracks where the wind had blown drifts to make their tracks deeper. They treasured these moments of pristine nature always.

While Kim had sisters with children, they all lived far away. Danny, Kim, and Dustin were the only ones on Kim's side who still lived in Cleveland. Dustin was the only boy on Danny's side. Danny's father easily made a big deal over Dustin. They went squirrel hunting, fishing, and tinkering with cars. Fishing was good in those parts. He and Papaw George would go fishing for crappie pronounced "craw pee." Some folks pronounced it "crappy." They say this is to prevent the rest of the world from knowing how good it was to eat!

The patch of woods where Danny grew up hunting with his father is still there, and back when he was young, it was a big deal to get a six squirrel limit. Danny and his dad went out trying to 'hunt' purely for the fun of it. They never did catch but one or two at the most for sport, so it didn't matter to them when the bag limit went up to ten and the number of the squirrels in the woods went up as well. Dustin enjoyed going squirrel hunting with his Papaw maybe even more than Danny did.

The *Cleveland Daily Banner* even had a good recipe for Squirrel Croquettes a long time ago.

"Cook eight small squirrels in salt water until the meat starts to fall off the bone. Remove the squirrels and allow to cool. When cool, remove the meat from the bones and shred. In a large bowl, combine the meat, onion, celery, salt, pepper, breading and milk. Mix well. Place in the refrigerator for one hour. Remove it from the fridge and shape into patties. Add some oil to a large skillet and heat over medium heat. Add the patties and cook

until light brown. Flip when half done. Serve and enjoy."

Kim could never do that -- she didn't have it in her. She shopped at the Bi Lo grocery store.

One of Dustin's favorite meals was Kim's recipe for chicken and dressing. Just hearing about the recipe would make your mouth water and your stomach begin to growl. It was a simple delicious idea. She just boiled a whole chicken until the meat came off the bone. Then she de-boned it. After that she put the chicken in the bottom of a casserole dish. In order to give it a moist creamy texture, she put a can of cream of chicken soup and a can of cream of celery soup on top of that. Next she poured on a package of Pepperidge Farm stuffing. Finally, a cup of chicken broth with one stick of melted butter was gently poured over the dry bits of stuffing. The creation went in the oven at 350 degrees for one hour or until the top was golden brown. This was just the thing Dustin loved to eat when he came home from squirrel hunting.

In Cleveland snow is rare. Snow is usually so minimal, the area isn't prepared for it and locals admittedly can't drive in it. The snow is very wet and freezes over quickly, making nasty ice patches. However, this is perfect for children and parents who can seize the moment and gather up enough snow to make a snowman.

When Dustin was growing up, schools often closed with even a hint of snow. One of those times there was actually enough snow to build a snowman. Kim, Danny and Dustin knew just what to do. They decided to take time out to play in the snow. Mother Nature had her say. The roads were blocked and they couldn't go anywhere, anyway. It was a good time for a trip out the front door and into the winter wonderland. Dustin yanked his hat over his ears and tied a scarf around his neck. Kim made sure he buttoned up his warm winter coat and grabbed his mittens before he rushed out. The fresh fallen snow had trimmed the trees with icicles. It was as if the bushes were frosted like cupcakes. The white snow glistened in the sunlight and Dustin felt the excitement of the newness. He made a snowball. He patted it in his hands, and it packed rather nicely. It was not too wet and not too dry. He came up with a plan. Just as Danny came out on the porch, Dustin hurled a snowball like it was a baseball and hit him square in the chest. That was it the war was on. The snowball fight had begun.

After a while the three of them decided to make a snowman! From all the stories he had read, he knew the proper way to make the big bottom snowball, as well as creating a classic snowman face.

The type of snow needed was perfect that day. The once in a lifetime moment of sledding, snowball fights, fort building, and angel making or rabbit tracking is so important to Cleveland children who rarely see much snow. Few people are snow experts, but Danny was. Angel-making needs the dry, powdery snow so that when you lay down in it and swish your arms around, it will dust off when you stand up again. Snowman snow, in terms of consistency, needs to be heavier, clumpier and moist. Just as there are different types of ingredients for baking a cake, there are different types of snow. You don't make brownies the same way you'd dust sugar cookies for decoration. Similarly, neither can you build a snowman with just any kind of snow.

When Dustin tested the snow, it felt just right. He scooped up a handful and tried to make a snowball. Since he was able to make a good, tight snowball, then it must be time to build a snowman! That particular day a delicate balance had been made: The snow was wet enough to be sticky, and it wasn't slushy. The magic of that moment, so rare in Cleveland was his.

There was the right amount of snow on the ground. It was more than the light dusting that Dustin had seen before. A little dusting was too difficult to roll enough snow together to build a snowman. They had waited until there were at least a few inches of the white stuff. The time had come. The sparkling sunlight reflected the glistening, magic, white snow. It was so bright you almost had to wear sunglasses.

Nothing seemed impossible that day. It all started with that first snowball, which he put on the ground and started rolling around the tree. More snow accumulated on the snowball as he pushed it around, until it got big enough to start the snowman. When the bottom ball got big, he pushed it towards its final resting place right in the front yard for Mom and Dad to see. He repeated the process for the middle ball, only made it smaller. He was glad he did when it came time to try to hoist it up onto the bottom ball.

Kim looked on as the crisp cold air nipped at her nose. She was present if Dustin needed help. Dustin was done making the middle ball, then realized it was too heavy to lift. They became so focused on the task of making the snowman that they did not hear the little tap on the front door from the cardinal eating the breadcrumbs they had left on the ridges of the frame for fun. Every peck at the crumbs made a little tap. The squirrels nearby heard it and looked past Kim, Danny and Dustin. They were focused on their task at hand of finding food in a world newly covered with snow. The weight of the outside snow almost muffled any outside noise. The tapping echoed in the warm kitchen, but no one was there to hear it except the dog. Why? Because Kim was right outside with Dustin. He needed help hoisting the center up onto the bottom. Kim grabbed her gloves from her pocket and put them on. With three pushes it was up and on top of the mound.

Together they made the snowball for the head the smallest of the three, but not too small. The fun part had just begun. Whew! This snowman making business was hard work. Now for the nose... They paused. Kim went in and pulled out a carrot from the refrigerator. Dustin snapped a twig in two and said "Now I have the arms!" They used Oreo cookies for eyes and M & M's to make a mouth. Kim and Dustin took a step backwards and thought to themselves that their snowman needed a hat. They went inside and rummaged through the front hall closet. Easy peasy, lemon squeezey! They found the perfect hat and scarf that had not been used before. They dressed the snowman, stood back, and looked one more time. The snowman was done!

They followed a classic design when building their snowman. Their creation stood, completed, right in front of the wood pile next to the house. They stabilized him at the bottom by jamming a broom into the snow underneath one of the arms.

At the top, it was sufficient just to lean the middle section of the snowman against the branch.

After the snowman was done, they shoveled the snow from the door and scraped and cleared the snow off the steps. The excitement was starting to die down and a cold chill was settling in on them a bit. Dustin felt like an icicle. He and Kim trudged back into the house and built a fire in the fireplace. They took off their shoes, put on warm dry socks and sat on the couch in front of the fire and cuddled, warm and snugly. Once they were warm enough and their cheeks were no longer numb, Kim sent Dustin out to get some snow for snow cream. They put milk and vanilla and sugar on top of the snow and then ate it. A pinch of salt would make it taste just right.

They sat there feeling the blood rush into their frozen fingers and toes as they gazed out the window. A snowflake drifted past them, then another, and another. They watched as the winter sun shone through the icicles and glistened on their freshly made snowman. It was a moment like this that stayed with them forever.

The snow kept falling that winter. Flake after flake piled upon flake after flake. It seemed so infinitesimal when you watched it for minutes at a time, but when you looked out again, the places you had walked upon were once again entirely covered. A fresh blanket of snow tucked you in and muffled the sounds of cars, people, and nature. The rabbits didn't like this, since their food was covered up, too. They had to forage from a wider range and predators could see where they were going. They could no longer keep their presence hidden when they snuck out and wandered about.

Soon Danny was home and they were sitting down to dinner with Dustin's favorite chicken casserole. The phone rang. It was Papaw George. He was so excited about the snow and wanted to remind Danny to show Dustin the rabbit tracks. Dustin was already in his pajamas, so he postponed it for the morning. Danny woke Dustin up at 6:00 a.m. and they were able to see where the rabbits went. Dustin saw this as two opportunities. The first opportunity was to miss school and the second opportunity was to catch a rabbit and finally see what rabbit stew tasted like. Both opportunities were dashed to the wind.

First of all, Dustin had lost total track of time. Dustin forgot it was Saturday morning, and he didn't have school. Secondly, Kim's favorite animal was the rabbit, and she had a collection of rabbit figurines on the windowsill that she admired. She liked rabbits because of their pure fluffy nature. She admired their cuteness, not their flavor. She had towels with rabbits, switch plates with rabbits, rabbit cookie jars, rabbit dishes, statues with rabbits, rabbit tea pots, and rabbit placemats. Dustin however loved to tease his mother about wanting to eat rabbit stew. He would never eat rabbit stew in front of her, because he knew how much she loved rabbits. In fact when he was seven years old he spent his first two weeks allowance he ever got on two decoratively sewn rabbits he bought at a garage sale. They had a price tag of $5.00. He wanted them so badly for his mama and told the neighbor that he would pay her the rest of the money later when he got paid again. She told him he could buy them for what he had, and so he paid three dollars. He delicately set them on the couch as if they were watching T.V. and then called his mother from the other room and said. "Mom I have some friends over watching T.V. that I would like you to meet." When she saw the cute well-dressed rabbits she was happily surprised. It touched her heart even more to know he used all of his money to buy them for her, so much that to this day those two rabbits are the most valuable possession Kim has.

As thoughtful as Dustin was, he would never miss a good opportunity to tease his mom. And so he continued to tease her, knowing full well that tomorrow's rabbit hunting expedition was for tracks only.

Rabbit footprints are unique in the way they are positioned. They have two footprints side by side at the front, one in the middle, and one at the back. The rabbit he tracked was moving left to right. Dustin delighted in how he could discover what the rabbit had been doing before he arrived. He looked carefully and saw claw marks in the footprints.

Finding those rabbit tracks in the still quiet of dawn helped Dustin appreciate all of the wonders God created. He connected to the Lord in a wide open way. Walking through the woods to admire one of God's creatures and the tracks they left behind was just one of the ways he did that.

7 LET'S PLAY BALL
ROLL on, thou ball, roll on!
Through pathless realms of space Roll on!

-William Schwenck Gilbert

The first time Dustin played any kind of sport with a group was T-ball. He loved T-ball. Kim loved to watch the children run back and forth across the field. There was so much energy, joy, and enthusiasm all bundled up in that tiny crowd of kids. All the kids would run to where the ball was. The ball would fly high in the air and the children would look up and run to it. It was like watching seagulls going after crusts of bread, only instead of squawks, there was laughter, shouts, and cheers.

From the time Dustin was three years old, he played baseball. Danny coached him until he started high school. He was a left-handed pitcher. When he was in T-ball he broke his arm. During each T-ball game he would hold that cast out and lay the bat on it, drop his arm and hit the baseball. He played 'T-ball' with a broken arm! It wasn't like he was actually doing the big thing, but he thought he was.

Danny seriously started coaching at Industrial Park and Blue Springs Ball Park. He started coaching Dustin in a more organized fashion now. He arranged practices, gear, uniforms, and registration fees. Dustin had a talent for sports and performed well on the field. In school he was not as motivated. He was a very smart boy, but he never liked to study. All the girls thought he was so cute.

Dustin learned teamwork. He perfected his physical skills. He learned the excitement of tactics and structure. Danny coached well. He taught those boys how to play baseball right. He was always boosting them up to try as hard as they could. He was a class act.

They did not win every single game, but they had the classiest coaches, parents and players. The negative roaring at the kids from the sidelines was not their style. They would instead use encouraging words. The boys played with respect for their teammates, opposition, and the umpires, no matter what. Danny had no plan but to get the children to play hard, well, and with dignity. When he wasn't coaching, he worked with Dustin by playing catch, throwing, practicing batting, and hitting ground balls every chance they could. He coached Dustin's teams all through elementary school. It was a great program, managed by Bradley County Parks and Recreation. The athletic programs at Blue Springs Park were wonderful too. Kids from four to fourteen years old could play. There were probably over 1,500 children in baseball in Bradley County. Kids' baseball was not as physical as football, but it could still be rough at times. Dustin slid into bases many times, causing skinned up arms and legs, requiring minor home medical attention. It was fun to see him up at the plate ready to hit that next line drive, or even possibly a home run.

The parents waited to see what the batter would do. This was where each boy got a chance to shine on his own. Every baseball position had its moments. Dustin liked pitching because he was good at it. The play always started with the pitcher. Watching him stand on the mound, only to glare at the batter ready to strike him out, was electric. All eyes focused on the pitcher at the start of each play of the game. Dustin was the pitcher. He was ready. All eyes were on Dustin.

They exposed Dustin to a variety of sports. They paid attention to Dustin's interest in a given sport to determine which sport he would play. Watching sports on television was a good

112

introduction. It was even more fun to watch a game in public and be a spectator in real life. Dustin's favorite teams were the Carolina Tar Heels for basketball and the Tennessee Vols for football. His favorite baseball team was the Atlanta Braves. Kim, Danny and Dustin went to several Atlanta Braves games. Dustin liked Fred McGriff and others.

They watched to see what sport Dustin would prefer. He decided it was baseball. He talked about the players, the strategies, and he told friends and family about the games he had watched. Soon he formulated his own personal preferences for baseball strategies and playing styles.

Dustin was a team player. He had an amazing pitching arm. He loved to throw a ball. He was best suited to baseball. He had tried multiple sports, but had narrowed it down to a few sports he enjoyed most. Danny taught him the fundamentals of baseball one on one. Danny spent hours with Dustin playing catch and having him field pop flies and grounders in the back yard. It was an annual ritual to go to get a physical from the doctor before participating in sports. Every year he was healthy and hearty except for the year he broke his arm. They had a neighbor, Tom

Kirkpatrick, who made the boys in the neighborhood catch one hundred pop flies each before they could go to dinner. Tom had a son named Jud who played with Dustin.

Coaching was more than volunteering, --it was a joyful hobby for Danny. He was a willing altruist who was committed to giving children of all abilities a chance to play baseball. He always had the idea in mind of building up their self-esteem. He carefully planned training sessions. He set goals and challenges that made it fun for everyone. Danny enjoyed watching how much Dustin enjoyed the game of baseball. Danny worked with all the boys all the time and motivated them to show up to training, ready to play. He made each child on the team feel like a born winner. He encouraged and helped them understand that winning the big shiny trophy was nice, but those small, personal achievements of playing your best and better than the week before was the way to get ahead. He did not pressure children to win a match through the threat of punishment. The best reason for playing was, not necessarily to win the league trophies, but to try their hardest. They played because it was fun, it was a great game, and they loved it.

Through baseball, Dustin learned responsibility and self-discipline. As a parent and a leader, Danny presented the best parts of himself to the children. It was quite an undertaking to be a coach. It required quite a commitment. Practicing at home, keeping track of equipment, coming on time to practices and games, and being active required a sacrifice of time and other interests. It was work to be a coach and keep everyone happy. He had to consider; how much play time each child got, when to play each child, when to take him out, how to allow each child a chance to breathe, and how each child can best develop new skills. When a Danny managed to balance these plays and keep each child engaged it was surprising even to Danny how well his team of individuals would improve upon their game.

When there were fewer ranting parents pressuring their children to win at all costs in baseball, Dustin and his teammates were given a chance to really play ball. Danny kept encouraging Dustin. He gave Dustin the opportunity to be on so many teams. Soon, the game came natural to him.

Danny and Kim worked with the parents to create a positive atmosphere for the kids. After every practice and game, Dustin came home with the deep red Tennessee dirt ground into his pants. He liked to slide into everything, even when he didn't have to. He liked to get his pants dirty, but the stains were hard to get out. Kim discovered that using Coca-Cola was the best way to remove those stains. Kim shared her recipe with the other moms. She and Danny made many long lasting friendships at those games.

The parents backed Coach Danny up and reassured their children by telling them after a game "I loved watching you play. It was great fun." This allowed the players to move on from mistakes and bask in the glow brought about by playing a physical, technical, social, and psychological, and competitive team sport. The team members knew that their parents all wanted them to become the best players they could possibly be. Danny created an environment for them to succeed, unhampered by a fear of failure.

Kim and Danny had patience to take the good with the bad. They took time out of their lives to explore all sports with Dustin, to practice and teach him new skills, to support him in his choices. Dustin started playing basketball with a community league in between his baseball fun during the winter months. Dustin learned Karate when he was five and six years old. For some, Karate can serve as a bullying prevention skill. But Dustin was never bullied. He was well-liked. He was the AAU (Amateur Athletic Union) champion in Georgia. Dustin had great reflexes. He was quick on his feet and was a natural at it. As a result, he earned his yellow belt before he gave up karate. The Karate gave him a great sense of self-esteem. He also liked basketball, but not as much as baseball. All of the sports were worth it. Their devotion to sports brought them closer together as a family.

As the years went on, baseball became more competitive. They knew the game's rules and respected the ump's calls most of the time. After all, Danny had been coach all through elementary and middle school. They made the commitment of time and money, they supported the team. They stayed humble when Dustin played well. They enjoyed every minute of his success. They always kept their thinking positive. Dustin was conditioned to achieve. Every year they prepared early and bought all their equipment before the prices were jacked up.

Sports intrigued Dustin. He was accustomed to letting his enthusiasm and energy he channeled into sports guide him. One day this interest led him to parts unknown. Kim and Dustin were walking around the block waiting for Danny to come home so they could go square dancing. Dustin asked if he could watch the big boys playing basketball. When Kim went out to get him, the big boys had gone and Dustin was nowhere to be seen. That totally terrified her. She called the police. It was getting darker. Neighbors heard and came out and started shining headlights and looking in the ponds. They asked Kim what Dustin had been wearing, but she couldn't be specific. His bicycle was found in a yard around the corner from his house in this relatively new subdivision. Danny came home and joined in the search going door to door asking neighbors if they had seen Dustin. Someone knew that the boys were playing basketball at an elementary school nearby. So, Danny quickly got in his car and drove to the school as fast as he could. He swung open the front doors and rushed in. A janitor directed him to the front office. When Danny got to the office, Dustin was there confused about what to do next. He ran to his daddy and said "I didn't know we were going to go so far, daddy."

Dustin liked to live "wide open and do life big." Everyone kept having to tell him to slow down. It was as if he heard a little voice inside saying "Spread your wings out wide." It seemed there were blue skies where he ran. He was so passionate about his game that everyone could feel his heart beat as he ran on the baseball field. He was fearless and loved sports. He just wanted to love, and give, and be happy every chance he could. The sun that shined on the Ledford family at that time included God's grace and love.

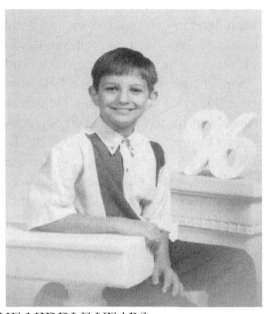

8 THE MIDDLE YEARS

"If God be for us, Who can be against us?"
- Romans 8:31

Fourth grade was a trying year for the
Ledford household. There was a major league
baseball strike. This was the eighth work
stoppage in baseball history.

For Dustin it meant that their family had to find something else to do on Sunday nights after church. All of the stats that Dustin had studied and applied his newly acquired math skills on were now useless speculations. The strike began on August 12, 1994 and resulted in the remainder of that season being cancelled. This didn't seem fair to Dustin. He certainly wanted to see the postseason games, and they were cancelled, too. This was a surprise to everyone and hadn't happened in his lifetime or even Grandpa's lifetime. It made him question the World Series as well as the world. Finally the strike was over on April 2, 1995. Hundreds of games had been cancelled. That didn't stop his love of baseball. He practiced his pitching skills in the backyard instead. Due to the strike, or maybe out of curiosity, Dustin did consider trying another sport.

In fourth grade, Dustin said he wanted to try football, and went to all the practices. At the first game, a boy cleated him in the thigh and he decided football wasn't for him. Football season was not as exciting as baseball for Dustin, Kim, or Danny. Although Dustin was a take-charge kind of guy who was up for any fun, he was wise to the pile-ups that broke many kids' collarbones. Kim usually made him finish what he started, but this time she let him quit, because she didn't like how rough and violent the game was, and she didn't want Dustin to get hurt. They were careful to expose Dustin to what he could handle.

Some days were not perfect. As the years went on late elementary and middle school was awkward for Dustin, as it was for so many. Some days he felt like he could do nothing right. But somehow his smile shined through to light up the room. He brought joy to the center of it all. He didn't just play sports, he played sports with heart and enthusiasm. Sometimes he would lay awake at night wondering about what it would be like to grow up. Most of the time he lived in the moment. There would be days when he didn't like school, or things didn't go the way he wanted, but in general, he was always a happy kid. He was truly present and accounted for with his bright smile.

Sports made school fun for Dustin, even if he did break his arm at the skating rink. It was junior high school. The coach called Kim and said "Come meet me at the emergency room. I think Dustin has broken his arm. But, don't worry. It is not his pitching arm." Luckily it wasn't, so he could still pitch after that. Once again he was under his favorite Carolina Tar Heels blanket snuggling up to the dog and convalescing on the couch fighting the pain of a broken arm.

It was at this same time in life they thought he could handle learning more about his biological mother. Kim and Danny asked Dustin if he wanted to meet his birth mother, but he had never wanted to meet her. He said Kim and Danny were the only parents he had ever known. Kim was grateful for that.

When Dustin was still in fourth grade, Kim wrote to the Sellers Adoption Services Home where she had given up her birth daughter, and told the Home that she didn't want her daughter to have to get a court order to open up the birth records. She gave them all the information she could, along with her current address, and her married name. She gave permission for them to give her information to the adoptive family.

So after 18 years, Kim's daughter's adoptive parents gave her that information for her high school graduation present. Her adopted parents had named her Brandi, and she wanted to meet Kim. They lived in Baskin, Louisiana, and came to meet Kim, Danny, and Dustin. Dustin and Brandi had an immediate bond. They met on May 24, Memorial Day weekend, 1994. That summer Kim took Dustin and Brandi to the beach in Biloxi, Mississippi and spent a week. They had a glorious time. Brandi came to see Kim several times. They still try to see each other once or twice a year. Brandi is married now, with two blond, blue-eyed girls.

If you were to ask Kim if she is Brandi's mother, she would deny it. She had never tried to be a mother to her. Anybody can be a mother but not everyone can be a "Mamma." Kim was the one who was there for Dustin. Bobbi was the one who was a "Mamma" for Brandi. Kim gave birth to Brandi, but Tim and Bobbi Eubanks in Baskin, Louisiana are her parents. Kim is Dustin's "mamma" and was always there for him. If you asked Kim if she felt like Brandi was her daughter she would say that she loved her and cared about her, but knows in her heart that Tim and Bobbi Eubanks are her parents. They raised her and she is their daughter. She is grateful to them for raising her and giving her the good life she had.

Likewise, Danny was Dustin's father. He was the one who coached his sport teams, played catch with him in the back yard and was always involved in his life. Danny and Dustin built a tree house in the back yard. There was a slab of concrete in the old house where they put Dustin's footprints. They tore it up and brought it to the new house when they moved.

There is something about a tree that just begs a kid to climb it. For Dustin, climbing a tree was more than just fun (although, ultimately, that's what made it so appealing). Scaling a tree taught him vital lessons, such as dexterity, risk assessment, focus, and planning. Dustin had regular practice climbing the oak tree in front of Grandma's house. He would climb so high that he was out of sight. He had to decide how high he was comfortable climbing, the best way to get there, which branches looked sturdiest, and figure out how to get back down. A successful climb built confidence, gave him a sense of freedom, and helped him appreciate nature. An unsuccessful climb had the most valuable lesson a child can learn: how to pick himself up and get right back at it again.

Kim and Danny were both there for Dustin in both happy and sad times, broken bones, skinned knees, and Santa Claus. When Dustin was six, he climbed a magnolia tree. When he got to the top he said "Mom, I can't get down from here." Kim said "You figured how to get up, now you figure how to get down." So he tried but fell forward on a hard limb as he was going down and broke his nose. The day after he fell out of the tree, he was still running around looking for the most exciting thing to do next. As always, he loved to go go go.

If you're new to tree climbing, be sure to start small. Climb up a few branches, then climb back down. Climbing is fun, getting stuck – not so much. We are always in search of good climbing trees. You know what would be awesome? A tree climbing directory. How cool would it be to be able to search for trees that are just begging to be scaled (http://theriskykids.com/2013/06/50-dangerous-things-you-should-let-your-kids-do-climb-a-tree/, by Angie Six, December 15, 2015)

Dustin couldn't always find a tree to climb when he really wanted one, so he would climb on a roof, or a bridge or anything he could get his hands on. Dustin was a hands-on kind of boy. Did he play with fire? Yes! There was an old wives' tale that said if you play with fire, you will wet the bed. Kim told him that story for safety sake! Did he drive a car? Yes! He and his father restored a 1989 white Chevrolet Camaro. It had T-tops. He drove to school and everywhere. Did he own a pocketknife? Yes! He had all kinds of pocket knives. His grandmother got him a Swiss Army knife. He was always whittling. One time they went to Applebee's and he was carving his name in the table. His mother nearly died of embarrassment. When he was ten years old he wanted to carve a pumpkin on his own. Danny and Kim didn't want to let him, but finally agreed.

While attempting to carve the eyes out on Halloween night, the knife slid and cut four of his fingers.

Despite the occasional danger of having hands on experiences Dustin was prepared for life. He lived life wide open and clung to the freedom given him. He embraced the world with his whole heart. He rode his bicycles without a helmet, because they weren't required then. He played in the neighborhood woods all day long. Kim always knew where he was and was always nearby. He would return home happy and well oxygenated for dinner refueling.

His experiences provided learning, and believe it or not, safety. He had so many cuts, scrapes, bruises, and sometimes broken bones. But he knew the world. He lived whole heartedly. He was given the chance to tinker, explore and experiment. He was prepared to do something very brave and big in the world. He had so much experience touching, and feeling the world and being in it. He knew what it was like to lick a battery and feel the sting on his tongue. He could throw rocks farther than any other boy in the neighborhood. He could drive a nail through a two by four in ten seconds flat. He knew how to make a slingshot and could ping a squirrel at 10 feet! He and Danny made a potato cannon made out of PVC. There was a switch that you flicked.

He could shoot a potato one hundred yards. You would hear it SWOOOSH through the air. You put lighter fluid in the plastic tube cannon and when you flicked the little switch, it ignited the fluid to force the potato to shoot out the end of the cannon. Many people still make these by following the instructions at (www.instructables.com/id/The-Original-**Potato-Cannon/**),

He knew what it felt like to stick his hand out the window when his parents were driving down the freeway at 60 miles an hour. He would always talk about flying! He would move his hands up and down and pretend he was flying. He super-glued his fingers together once. He was always into something. He saved mementos from his escapades playing, in the air-conditioning ductwork. Tucked inside those ducts was a treasure trove of money and knick-knacks, rocks, and plastic toy army men.

Throughout his life growing up Kim and Danny gave Dustin as many hands on experiences as they could. Dustin squashed pennies upon the railroad tracks in Stone Mountain, Georgia's railroad attraction. He loved to sleep in the forest overnight. After baseball games on Friday night, boys would come over and sleep on the living room floor or camp outside. The treehouse Danny and he built would come in handy for overnights. One night they even slept on the trampoline. Dustin made forts under the kitchen table. He loved playing in his fort. He had many secret hiding places. He liked to play with fireworks. He liked to experience the excitement of the stuff of life. He loved riding his go cart or his motorcycle.

Kim and Danny also gave Dustin a religious education. Dustin knew what he was about and was always close to God. One day in the summer after fourth grade, he came home from Vacation Bible School and recited a passage from the Bible that from then, on, he quoted regularly to everyone. It was II Timothy 1:7 *"For God has not given us a spirit of fear but of power and might and a sound mind."* Dustin knew in his own mind that he believed in God the Father and he believed in Jesus Christ. That summer he learned to believe in the Resurrection and that Jesus is coming back again.

Weeks later Dustin woke up and was afraid he was going to die and go to hell. When he told Kim, she called Pastor Brenton Cox from Valley View Baptist Church. He came over right away and sat in the living room and asked if Dustin was ready to be saved. Pastor Cox looked into his eyes and said "Do you know what sin is? Did you know that Jesus died to save you from your sins?" Dustin answered "yes." Dustin asked the Lord Jesus Christ to come into his heart. His face looked so proud after that. He joyfully wanted to share his faith with his mother and father.

He sang with more conviction at church after that. He sang anthems, hymns, and more, but in his heart he knew the Lord more strongly than that. Dustin was certainly not a "perfect" child. He had many weaknesses and temptations. As he got older he never stopped believing in the Holy Spirit and he knew that God was giving him new life. Kim knew he might feel lost at certain times in his life, but after that summer, she was assured that Dustin had faith and a foundation from which to begin his walk with God. She rejoiced in this and once again knew God's love would never fail.

9 HIGH SCHOOL SWEETHEARTS

"No sooner met but they looked; no sooner looked but they loved; no sooner loved but they sighed. No sooner sighed but they asked one another the reason; no sooner knew the reason but they sought the remedy."

- Shakespeare, <u>As You Like It</u>, Act V, Scene 2

Dustin was not aware of exactly how charming he was. His tan, fresh face and sparkling, green eyes conquered many a young girl's heart. He became more aware of his charm the day he came to school after breaking his arm at baseball practice. His buddy helped him carry his lunch to the table. They sat and talked about the team for a while until Lauren, Nicole, or Fawn, or maybe another girl came up to him and said "What happened to your arm? Can I sign your cast?" The signing requests and sympathy did not stop. It did help to soften the pain from the broken bone, though.

Dustin's tree climbing experience paid off when it came time to impress his friends. He always kept an eye out for trees or any good climbing candidates. That was just his nature. It was as if he was noting where they were so that when the urge to climb came about again, he would know right where to find them. He thoughtfully spared sharing these spots with those who were afraid of heights. But he was sure to share climbing places with his friends, and together they would go out to the most wonderful spots in nature in groups that included boys and girls, and have a great time.

Dustin was taught to respect women. At a high school dance or prom, he treated each of his dates with respect. He bought the nicest corsages, opened doors, and complimented the young ladies. Kim was proud that he treated girls well.

The friends he hung around with felt safe with Dustin. They trusted he would protect them just enough, yet find fun adventurous things to do. He knew all the best places to jump into the river, and branches to swing from. They always called him when they went to swim in the river because he was a life guard.

Lauren was Dustin's girlfriend in fifth grade. Lauren went to a dance with him in middle school and she was taller than Dustin. Dustin also played with Lauren's little sister, Rachel, as they were really just good friends.

After Lauren, Keari became his girlfriend. She was a cheerleader in junior high. Just for fun, Dustin put on her cheerleading uniform and they took hilarious pictures which sure did get a lot of laughs.

In ninth and tenth grade he dated Nicole. She was always studying and encouraging Dustin to do the same, but to no avail. Danny, Kim and Dustin would often go to Nicole's parents' house and play cards. They liked to play Rook. Nicole would get upset because Dustin would go outside and play basketball with Zack, Nicole's little brother often.

In eleventh grade Dustin took another Nicole to the prom. She was a year older than Dustin. Her dress was a long creamy white dress. Dustin wore a black tuxedo.

In twelfth grade he dated a little blond girl (the first blond he ever dated). Leah played basketball for McMinn County. He took her to the prom. She wore a long black dress, and he wore a white tux with tails.

He liked to give these girls rings with their birthstones on them. He was sentimental that way. He liked the girls, and the girls liked him. Even in that awkward stage when he was not quite as tall as the girls, he could still charm them. Kim still has the picture of Dustin dressed up at the dance with Lauren McKay. She towered over him by at least eight inches, with her high heels. He was wearing a dapper sweater to match her black sparkly dress. Kim always gave Dustin the money to pay for the dance tickets, the refreshments, the corsage, or the pictures. She was old fashioned in the belief that a gentleman should treat his date like a lady and pay for the evening's entertainment. Kim noticed the money in his pants pocket when she was doing laundry after the dance. When he came home after baseball practice after school she asked him where he got the money from. He told her that Lauren started to pay for everything, and he figured he might as well keep that money for fun for later. Kim was shocked. She made him call and apologize to Lauren and forced him to bring the money to her at school the next day. She wanted him to learn from her how a lady should be treated.

10 COACH!

"Go call a coach and let a coach be called; And let the man who calleth be the caller. And in his calling let him nothing call but Coach! Coach! Coach!"

–Henry Carey, Chrononhotonthologos

There comes a time for parents when they realize that the child they have guided, molded, encouraged, cheered and motivated needs some new guidance. It feels both good and bad, knowing in their hearts that this child has a life apart from theirs, full of joy, strength, knowledge, skills and motivation all his own; he will do what he will, have what he shall, and be what he is. He is a person all unto himself. It is sad for a parent to realize that their days of major influence are ebbing, and nothing can be done to stop that tide.

This moment arrived when Danny's coaching days were laid to rest and Dustin had a new Coach. By the time Dustin got to high school, he knew more about baseball than Danny did, so Danny had nothing left to teach him. This didn't stop the attention or the cheering. It was different for Danny now. His now sat on the cold bleachers, as a spectator. He sat there, unmoved on the outside, thinking through each play, throw, run, and umpire call. Kim always sat beside him with a thermos of hot chocolate and a blanket, on the coldest of the cold days. Even after Danny stopped coaching they still went to tournaments, spring ball, fall ball, and Cocoa Beach Florida for one week in the spring for camp. They went to all the games and tournaments.

Once Dustin got to high school, they let the coaches be coaches. They did not argue with the umpire or scream at their kid like some parents. They stuck around for practices and were prepared to help if the coach asked, and kept out of his way if not asked.

Kim and Danny sat in the bleachers with their black and gold scarves. There were just over four hundred students in Dustin's graduating class, so it was a small town and the games were small to. It was easy to get to know everyone. The home team pride bonded them together even more. The school's mascot was the Bradley Bear and the school colors were black and gold.

After playing sports all through elementary, middle, and high school, Dustin had so many T-shirts in his closet. He never wanted to part with them because they held so many memories for him, even though they no longer fit. Kim had his uniforms from the three-year-old T-ball player to the uniforms of the 6'1" senior baseball player. After Dustin graduated and wasn't playing sports as frequently, it was time to put closure on his high school years. It was time to use her talents as a great seamstress. Kim gathered up the shirts and decided to make a T-shirt quilt. This was a perfect way to turn a batch of old shirts into permanent memories and Dustin was kind enough to part with a select number of the shirts.

Kim decided on the basic square design with a backing of fabric with a pattern of baseballs and gloves. She cut off the sleeves, then cut below the neck banding and above the bottom hem of each shirt. She trimmed each shirt until she had a perfect square panel, and then cut each square to an equal size. It was going to be a warm and comfortable quilt. She carefully ironed and starched each square for stability. She used interfacing to firm up the stretchy, elastic, cotton fabric, and sharp scissors to cut and make the panels. She placed sashing between the T-shirt panels with cornerstones to help separate the squares and increase their size. She had a nice simple design that brought years and years of sports together on this one canvas.

She had a T-shirt from his Bradley Central High School. He was a left-handed pitcher, Dustin was one of the fastest on his team at Bradley Central High School, where he graduated in 2004. He then attended Cleveland State Community College. Just like any boy, he played pranks, joked around and got in trouble. Kim and Danny had a hard time staying mad at him because of his beautiful smile. He was the greatest joy they ever had.

She had his School T-shirt. Dustin was consistently an A or B student. He could have been an "all A" student, if his heart had been into academic study. He preferred to be outdoors. Mother Nature was his teacher and the fields and streams were his notebooks and blackboards. He was smart, but did not want to study for long periods of time.

She only put baseball T-shirts in this quilt even though Dustin loved water. When he first learned how to waterski he was fearless. He fell only two times before he was easily holding onto the lead behind the motorboat on the Hiwassee River. He would go to a rope swing on Parksville Lake, which was up in a tree on a bank. He climbed up the bank, then onto the tree, grabbed the rope and swung into the lake. On Saturdays and Sundays Dustin could be seen on the Hiwassee, or the Tennessee River, doing "doughnuts" and other tricks with his burgundy and white jet ski.

She didn't even save the T-shirt from the the Life Center. Dustin started working when he was fifteen years old. He was a lifeguard at First Baptist Family Life Center. Since Kim worked there, Dustin was allowed to work at the Center at a much younger age. He did a great job of life-guarding. When he was sixteen, he got a job at their city recreation pool, and worked there for about three years. It was a great job for him because he was able to handle that and baseball as well. He was proud of being able to keep people safe in threatening weather.

There was the time when Dustin saved a little boy at Tinsley Pool. He was at his post on the deep end, and there was a life guard posted at the five foot area. Dustin saw the boy go under, ran from his post, dove in, and got the little boy out of the water immediately. Even though he got in trouble for leaving his post, that was how Dustin was -- a man of action. He responded to the moment, as if by instinct.

Dustin was always ready to jump in and save people. Most of the time it worked out. There was one particular painful time when it did not. One night, Dustin went to a party, and saw a young man beating up his girlfriend. Dustin tried to stop him, and got hit in the back of the head with a baseball bat. It caused three brain bleeds, and he spent three days in ICU at Erlanger Hospital in Chattanooga, Tennessee.

His Parksville Lake T-shirt was long worn out and could not be used in this quilt. His friends admired him for his sense of justice, and strength, and they trusted he would always protect them when they went to the Ocoee river. He and his buddies used to go up to the Ocoee River and go body surfing, and river rafting. They always wanted him to come along because he was a confident swimmer. The Ocoee River fed into Parksville

Lake where the rope swing was. All of Dustin's crowd used to go river rafting together and everyone made sure they were with Dustin, because he was a life guard and they felt safe with him.

His mission trip T-shirt was a memory to be fond of too. Dustin loved to be around children. He went on church mission trips, he played baseball with the little boys, and he participated in Backyard Bible Club. Kim treasures the picture of Dustin with two of the boys. On one mission trip to New York, he was at the World Trade Center, just two months before the September 11, 2001 tragedy.

Kim had enough T-shirts to make several quilts, but she had to choose a theme. She knew baseball would have to be the theme of this quilt. Then some day she would make another quilt perhaps.

11 A WORLD OF WORK

*"No man is born into the world whose work is not born
with him. There is always work, and tools to work withal,
for those who will; And blessed are the horny hands of toil."*

–James Russel Lowell

Dustin was a natural outdoorsman. He
especially enjoyed the construction profession
because he could be outside in the sunshine and
fresh air. He loved Cleveland with its streams and
creeks and rainbows that peaked out from the
clouds when the sun shone through the rain. He

did home repairs and roofing when he first started working full time after graduation from high school, and liked to use his hands. His grandfather had taught him so much all those years in his shop.

One year, Dustin worked for a tent company and went to Kentucky to put up a tent. Unfortunately, he disliked that job, and lasted only one summer. He always came back home to Cleveland, though, where Mom and Dad were. Cleveland is a small town, but you can't miss it from Interstate 75. There are only three exits on Interstate 75 -- Knoxville on the North, and Chattanooga to the South, but Dustin never passed the exits to Cleveland.

Papaw George thought Dustin might inherit the family business. Dustin thought about that as he got older. The plusses to this job were obvious. Dustin could work on his own vehicles as pet projects and it would cost less. An experienced mechanic could make decent money. Nevertheless, the hours required would be unlimited and taxing. Winter would be hard working in the shop. Tools were expensive, and one had to keep up with the technology. Sometimes the heat and cold could get to him. Hurting himself accidently was always a possibility, and Dustin had had plenty of experience with broken bones. Getting dirty was just part of the job. Dustin thought he would try something else, and Danny agreed. He knew there was something that would suit him better.

Dustin tried being an electrician. He didn't want to be a mechanic. Even though he enjoyed transforming the '89 Camaro, in the shop with Danny, he couldn't see himself doing that as a full time job. They worked hard together and had completely rebuilt it and had the interior done, all of the paintwork. and the result was beautiful. Dustin got a taste of the world of work at sixteen years old with this '89 tee-top Camaro. He was in heaven until somebody ran into him at a red light. It didn't hurt him but it damaged his car really badly. It was hard to see all that hard work destroyed.

The tried roofing three years after high school. His experience climbing fit this job well. Dustin had been on the roof with his Dad, fixing things, when he was three and four years old. So when later he became a roofer, he wasn't afraid of anything He could climb onto a roof as easily as a spider climbs an awning, earning the nickname "Spider Man" from his fellow workers. However, one day he forgot to tie himself off and he fell thirty feet off of a roof and broke his ankle. He was very fortunate that was all the damage, after a thirty foot fall.

Finally Dustin found something that suited him. He started working at Shane's Rib Shack. He loved barbeque and he loved people. Shane's Rib Shack had the kind of casual feel to it. The original owner was a sportsman just like him. The original shack was a tin roof building complete with an outhouse in Georgia. The chain has tried to keep that down home feeling that was part of the original restaurant. He enjoyed the family atmosphere. He gobbled up the food, and the sauces. He liked that they made everything from scratch. The ribs, the chicken, the fries, the okra were all part of a day's work for Dustin. He enjoyed working the late hours and meeting all the people. He saw a lot of his friends from Cleveland and enjoyed being around people. They were a nice family place.

12 SURPRISE!!

"Sport, that wrinkled Care derides, and Laughter holding both his sides. Come and trip it as ye go. On the light fantastic toe."

-John Milton

There was rarely a day a smile did not cross Dustin's lips. There was rarely a day a practical joke did not cross his mind. His smile was infectious, as was his laughter. He enjoyed a laugh for laughter's sake.

Dustin demonstrated his passion for a good

laugh on Mother's Day, 2006. This was just after he graduated, and had a new job at Hollister at Hamilton Place in Chattanooga. He didn't like that job as much as some of his other jobs, because this job was indoors folding clothes, and Dustin preferred being outdoors. Nevertheless, he was proud of the fact that he was earning his own money. He said "Here Mom. I got you something for Mother's Day." She said "You didn't have to get anything for me." He said "No, Mom, I wanted to. I wanted to get you something nice. I got a job. I got my own money now." Kim opened it and it was a heart necklace that said "Mom," and had a little diamond inside the letter "O." She loved it and treasured it more than anything. Dustin said he had another present, but would give it to her later. Kim told him that she didn't want him to go to too much trouble. She was so pleased with the necklace that she could not imagine anything better.

Most parents wait to go to bed until after their children are in for the night. For some reason that night, Kim went to bed before Dustin got home. Dustin snuck into their bedroom, took their Yorkshire Terrier, Bogey, out of the bed and put him in another room. He set up their video camera on the antique mantel on the opposite wall of their bed. He went into his bedroom and got his metal North Carolina Tar Heel garbage can and turned the video camera on and set it to record what was going to happen next. He then proceeded to light a whole string of fire crackers in that garbage can. Kim honestly thought somebody was shooting at them and she was dead. Just before the video cuts off, you can hear Danny say "When I get your mom off the top of me, I'm going to kill you!" Covers were flailing everywhere. Kim still has that video to this day. It is that type of peak experience that she'll never forget. Dustin lived that way.

14 LIFE'S LOVE

"That which we look on with unselfish love And true humility is surely ours, Even as a lake looks at the stars above and makes within itself a heaven of stars."

-Mary Gardiner Branard

While some say that love is just a word, Dustin found a way, a spark, and a lifeline to love passionately. He had many girlfriends in high school. He loved to shower them with gifts and make them feel loved and special, learning this from his parents. He bought birthstone rings for special girls he was dating. The many dances and many dates that he had gave him a chance to think about what he wanted in a woman, and as he grew up and matured, he learned more of what love was all about. But so far, none went so deep as to last too long.

Beautiful ladies dazzled Dustin, but Lyndsay was more than that. Lyndsay was the love of his life. He was a gentleman who appreciated women, but he more than appreciated Lyndsay. It was as if her voice sang to his soul. All those cheer leaders, river jumpers, dance partners, giggles, laughs and fun brought him joy, but Lyndsay did that and so much more. They had an understanding and a deep connection. He embraced the joy and showered the lovely ladies in his life with gifts in the past. But, with Lyndsay, every moment they spent together was a gift. He honored his past dates and treated them well. But there was something different about Lyndsay that made every experience they had seem fresh and new.

Dustin and Lyndsay first met on Halloween night in 2007 and fell in love. He loved Lyndsay and her daughter, Serenity. He became a man and loved and cared for his fiancé. He was someone she could call when she was down. He was a lifeline that lifted her up and allowed her to lay her troubles down for a while. If he thought that love was just a word, he wouldn't have done all the things he did. There was a spark he believed in that there would always be a way to make things right. Dustin, Lyndsay, and Serenity went on outings together.

One particular weekend stood out in their memories like a beacon of light showing them that they were now a unified family, full of love. They went to the Blue Hole off the Upper Ocoee River, with their sunscreen, towels, hats, and bug spray in the car. When Dustin told Serenity about the underwater tunnels, she was excited and wanted to know if she could jump in or use the goggles to look at the rocky bottom. Dustin said "I'm going to show you my favorite spot, and I know you won't be disappointed." He lovingly looked over to Lyndsay and assured her she could sunbathe, too.

When they arrived at the parking lot they grabbed all their gear and started their trek down the path leading to the swimming area. Serenity gasped with joy when she saw the underwater sinkhole. She dipped her foot in and found it cool from the running mountain waters. This Blue Hole was surrounded by a circular patch of water encompassed by rocks to sunbathe on. The peaceful, deep blue water held by rocks and greenery was a dramatic contrast. It was like a Monet painting, featuring dark blue, from the deep waters and the lighter blue of the shallows, surrounded by sunshine, trees, leaves, and olive colored Ocoee River water. As deep as it was, the blue light managed to reach the white sand and return rays of the sun's reflection.

They were having a glorious time. Lindsey was sunbathing on the warm rocks. Dustin and Serenity were in the water.

They saw a cluster of yellow butterflies.

It was as if they were absorbing minerals and nutrients from the puddles they were wading in. Here they were together, sharing the nurturing of the earth. Lyndsay was soaking up the sun's rays. Serenity was soaking up the attention Dustin gave her. Dustin was taking in the family time and the fresh mountain air.

The sunlight shimmered on the pools of water on the big rock. Occasionally they would climb up and jump off the big rock. It was a heavenly afternoon. Suddenly Lyndsay heard a loud splash and quickly Dustin handed Serenity to her. A snake had floated by. Dustin had reacted instantly. Although he spoke calmly, his eyes widened with excitement. That water moccasin had been sharing the water with them, and he had hoisted Serenity up onto the rock just in time, and then jumped up on the rocks himself. They had come so close to being bitten. They tried to relax and let the sun dry their cold, wet skin.

They glanced over at the next rock where there was a puddle of water, about the size of a rabbit, and a cluster of yellow butterflies wading in the muddy pool, with a cluster above moving back and forth. Two hundred butterflies surged in and out as if they were performing the dance of life. Everything was covered with yellow. They even landed on each one of the three now and then, and hovered around them. From then on, the butterfly was a sign of comfort to them. No sound, no commentary ruined this moment. Those bright yellow butterflies elegantly flapped their wings and turned and basked in the beams of light shining through the trees. It was hard to tell where one butterfly ended and the next one began. It was as if they were all part of the brilliant light that matched their bright yellow color. All the butterflies suddenly arose and continued to flock closer above them. They sensed that this was a magical moment that might never happen again. They all felt part of one another, like a family -- just as the butterflies appeared to be one beam of golden glowing light.

Dustin felt a familiar comfortable feeling with Lyndsay and Serenity. Serenity, Lyndsay, and

Dustin were like the family he came from. Just like Kim and Danny had Dustin in the center of their lives, he wanted to have Serenity in the center of his life with Lyndsay. This meant so much to Lyndsay. Kim always told Dustin that he had something special in the world to do. This made him rise above the average person. Other men had wanted Lyndsay all to themselves in their relationship with her. He rose above that sort of selfishness. Perhaps he knew there was more to life than that. His birth mother chose to give him up when she could have chosen otherwise. She knew God would use Dustin in mighty ways. Maybe his moment of shining would be with Lyndsay as he would be an awesome father for that little girl. He felt a special bond with them both.

15 EGGS AT MIDNIGHT

"Fly not yet; 'tis just the hour When pleasure, like the midnight flower. That scorns the eye of vulgar light, Begins to bloom for sons of night. And maids who love the moon. Oh stay, -- Oh Stay -- Joy so seldom weaves a chain like this to-night, that oh, 'tis pain To break its links too soon. Fly not yet."

–Thomas Moore

Two weeks after he saw the butterflies dance in the sun Dustin called Danny to wish him a happy birthday. They talked for about half an hour, and Dustin told him all about the butterflies, and how in love he was with Lyndsay. It was July 9, 2010. They said goodbye, and Danny set out to pack his suitcase for their trip to Calhoun, Georgia.

Danny and Kim went to visit their best friends who had moved to Calhoun. They went out to eat on that Friday night, doing the "cake and ice cream" thing. They went back to their condo, played cards, and eventually went to bed, planning to shop at the antique stores around Adairsville the next day.

Danny went to bed that night happy. He couldn't help but reflect on how proud he was of his son and how he embraced his new maturity. He saw how Dustin was fully attentive and committed to Lyndsay.

Meanwhile, that July night Dustin and Lyndsay wanted to arrange a late evening rendezvous. Lyndsay called Dustin at his friend's house and asked him to pick up some eggs and bacon on the way home. Dustin gladly went to the Super Walmart.

At about 1:30 Danny's cell phone rang. It was Dustin's girlfriend, Lyndsay, asking if Dustin was with them. Kim responded that they were in Calhoun, Georgia. Lyndsay then said "I think he's been in a wreck. I can't get him on his phone."

16 EMERGENCY!!

"It is by presence of mind in untried emergencies that native metal of man-is tested."

— James Russell Lowell

Kim and Danny knew they had to immediately head back to Cleveland to find out what was happening. They were on Interstate 75 within five minutes, and Danny drove.

How brave they were driving in the night to be there for Dustin. They did not know what was in store for them. They kept their minds on the task at hand, which was getting to their son.

Kim used her cellphone as if she were a radio operator in an all-out battle and started to make calls. She first called the hospital, and learned that indeed Dustin was there, but they could not elaborate further without proof of who she was. She said, "Is my son there?" They said "We can tell you he is here, but we can't tell you anything about his condition because we don't know you are who you say you are." Next, she called the Sheriff's department and asked "Could you please put me in touch with the officer who has worked my son's wreck?" In just one minute her cell phone rang. The officer told her his name. Kim said, "Can you tell me anything?" She got the same answer the hospital told her and quickly ended the call. In desperation, Kim called her neighbor who had a son two years younger than Dustin. They had grown up together from the ages of four and six. Kim told Becky the situation, and asked if she could go to the hospital and pretend to be his mother so she could find out more. By now, it was nearly two o'clock in the morning. It is a dear friend that can be called at 2:00 in the morning and will get up and go. Becky got up and was gone in two minutes flat. Kim was frantic. She wanted to know. Danny was torn up inside as he listened to the phone calls. Kim called her sister, Debby, told her the situation, and asked her to come. Again she said, "Dustin has been in a wreck and nobody will tell me anything that is going on. Will you please come?" Although her 86-year-old mother was there in Cleveland, Kim didn't want to call her and worry her.

When Kim and Danny got to Dalton they

took the Tunnel Hill exit. When you are coming up Interstate 75, you can cut off at Tunnel Hill and avoid Chattanooga. Kim called it the Cleveland Dalton highway. If you cut off that malfunction junction area where the two interstates I-24 and I-75 interstates combine in Chattanooga, and get back on I-75, you can get to Cleveland faster.

When they got to Dalton, Kim called the hospital again to find out how Dustin was. "Is there any chance my son is going to be airlifted to Chattanooga?" This was the closest trauma center at Earlanger. This news led her to believe that Dustin might still be alive, although they said "We don't know. The doctor is in there with him now." Her head had already been trying to tell her heart she actually feared that he was gone, but her heart didn't want to listen. Her thoughts flew back and forth as to whether he was going to be o.k. or not. When they told her that the doctor was still in there with him she thought to herself that he was still alive. She thought for a moment that it was going to be and he would survive this. But, she still felt inside that it wasn't going to be o.k. As much as she was trying to convince herself that it was going to be just another one of his injuries, she knew deep down that it wasn't the same. She never got the phone call that they were going to fly him to Erlanger, so they went ahead and exited at the Cleveland Dalton highway. About the time they crossed the Tennessee state line her cell phone rang again in the silence of the car. It was Becky, her neighbor. Becky said "Kim, was Dustin's wreck on APD 40?" but Kim didn't know. APD 40 forms a semi-circular bypass around Cleveland, connecting exits 20 and 25 on Interstate 75. There are two lanes going east and two lanes going west with a large median in-between. The speed limit is 55 there, and it covers almost the whole area of Cleveland.

Becky went on to explain that as she was heading to the hospital, she found traffic stopped going in both directions. When they started moving, she looked in her rearview mirror. "Baby," she said, "It's Dustin's car and it looks like a bomb went off." Kim and Danny were still twenty minutes from the hospital. By the time they got on APD 40, the officer that she had talked to earlier called to say "Ms. Ledford, have you been given an update on your son?" She said, "No, nobody will tell me anything." He said "I am sorry to tell you that your son has succumbed to his injuries in an automobile accident."

At that moment Kim wanted to scream. She wanted to run. She wanted to be anywhere but where she was in that automobile, hearing that news. She couldn't do any of that because right next to her was her ever-loving husband. She knew how much he loved Dustin and how this would kill him. She knew if she fell apart he would never get her to the hospital. At that very minute all she wanted to do was hold her baby even though she knew he was gone.

The officer told her that he was putting Chaplain William Lamb, who Danny and Kim knew, on the phone with her right then.

Danny kept asking her questions. She looked at Danny and said "Drive faster, drive faster!" He did. He drove from Calhoun to Cleveland in an hour, speeding as if he were a policeman in pursuit of a criminal. He heard her say "Yes, I know William Lamb." He was a good friend of theirs and was the clergy at the hospital that night. She knew that as long as she was talking, she could avoid Danny's questions, so she kept talking. William told her to get off of APD 40, because he didn't want her to pass the wreck site. He said " It looks like a bomb went off." She told Danny they had to get off, and continued to ignore his questions. As they approached the hospital, William told her to meet him at the back of the ER.

As Danny pulled up to a stop sign, there was a moment then that felt surreal. It was a moment that stood still and cut into their future and through their past like a dagger. It was the moment she had to tell Danny what had just been told to her. Kim had to tell him that Dustin was dead. Neither one of them could remember anything from that point, on. A numbness set in. A shock to their systems was coursing through their hearts and souls and bodies. Somehow they were rushed into that room that nobody ever wants to go in. They do not know how they got from that point to the back of the emergency room. It was as if angels picked them up and carried them, for they could not have walked alone.

When they got to the Emergency Room there were fifteen or twenty young people outside and as many inside. Through text messaging, Facebook, and My Space, they all knew immediately where he was and what had happened. Dustin was powerfully loved and had so many friends.

Among the crowd there was Dustin's girlfriend and her three-and-a-half-year-old daughter, Serenity, who Dustin had been "Daddy" to since she was nine months old. Serenity was a beautiful little brown eyed curly haired girl whose biological father was not in the picture. Dustin had stepped up and become a daddy to that precious little girl. Kim had to try to explain what death was to Serenity that night -- to a little girl who hadn't even lost a goldfish. Serenity didn't understand what death was, didn't understand that her Daddy was gone and that she was never going to be able to be with him again.

Kim had a funny feeling that night. Upon reflection, she knows there is no space that God's love can't reach, but her world felt emptied. In quiet moments of prayer now, she knows there is no end to His amazing grace, but at that time her world had fallen into an abyss. That phone call made the bottom drop out of her world. She refused to believe Dustin had passed.

At first she and Danny held on to the hope that Dustin could still be alive somehow. She kept holding on to his memory. She held on to the idea that maybe he would be able to pull through his injuries. After all, he had survived many broken bones before, and survived the fever he had as a baby, as well as the brain bleed that put him in the ICU. She held on to the memory of how athletic and strong he was, that he could withstand a crash. She held on to his positive disposition that helped him through so much before. It was in the middle of this anguish that she had to accept that he was not going to make it.

When she finally arrived at the hospital to see him one last time, she was not allowed to touch him or be near him, due to what they called an investigation. It would not have been right to let her see him until he had been cleaned up from what must have been an awful mess. She learned that his chest had to be cracked open for doctors to work on him. It would be days before Kim could see him.

They started to leave after three hours, but Kim knew she couldn't go home because Dustin still lived at home. Since her mother lived two blocks from the hospital, they went to her house. It was two weeks before they felt they could return home and face Dustin's bedroom and his belongings throughout the house. There are two Rubbermaid totes of clothes that Kim still has in her closet. Can there be any peace of mind when a parent loses a child? This is the untried emergency no one should ever have to bear. Kim and Danny endured this test. They believe to this day that it was only through the grace of God.

That Saturday morning, Kim's sister Debby told their mother the news that her youngest grandson had been killed in a car crash.

Kim and Danny did not know the details of the accident at that point. It didn't actually matter while they were making Dustin's final arrangements. There was no changing the course of time, no matter what had happened. All they knew was that their son was gone. On that Saturday they couldn't bring themselves to make funeral arrangements because their hearts were in so much pain.

Danny's birthday was on the ninth of July. Dustin got killed just after midnight on the tenth. That day Danny wandered about for a while. Then, since he ran his own business, he had to go to the shop and put up signs to announce that he would not be in for a while. He had to leave a new answering machine message to tell callers that he would not be back for at least two weeks.

We expect our children will bury us. This expectation had been dashed for Danny and Kim. Kim's sister made Dustin's funeral arrangements for her since she was emotionally unable to handle the task. Kim wanted to buy Dustin new clothes in which to be buried, even though she had four or five totes of his clothes already. Rick and Vickie Ownby from their church took Kim to American Eagle. Danny understood. The funeral home recommended a long-sleeve shirt, so they shopped for a long-sleeve shirt, a T-shirt, boxer shorts, a pair of khakis, and a belt. Mary Mantooch was the sales clerk in the store that day. Mary had just lost her son about two years before. In less than 24 hours God was already putting people in Kim's path who had lost a child and knew how to help her cope with this loss. Kim didn't know why they were not told to get shoes. She walked through the white wooden shelving, tables, and clothes racks. She held up wooden hanger after hanger, finding it difficult to select a fashionable long-sleeve shirt on this hot summer day. With tears streaming down her face, Kim found a nice plaid long-sleeve shirt, and tried to decide on a pair of Khaki pants. She knew Dustin's size by heart as he grew and changed. This would be the last time she bought clothes for him. She had to sit on a chair in the back of the store for a while, as grief overcame her. Images on the television were of no interest to her.

Someone placed their hand on her shoulder. The background music in the store played on, almost soothing her. Finally, she got up and was able to pick out the rest of his clothes. Somehow they got through that Saturday.

The following Sunday Kim's sister Debby asked her to go to the funeral home to look at what she had done, to make sure that everything was acceptable to her. Kim didn't remember much about what she had done. She didn't care about most of the details, but she remembered seeing a bed in the corner. Kim asked if that was the one that was selected for Dustin, but Debby explained that it was $1500 extra. Kim wanted that one, regardless of the extra price. The funeral director said he would give it to her without the additional cost. When she saw that it had baseball diamonds on all four corners, she knew that it was meant for Dustin, since baseball had been such a big part of his life. And Kim said "O.K."

On Sunday morning they went to the funeral home, signed all the paperwork, and finalized things. She gave the funeral director the clothes she had bought. He gently lifted the clothes tenderly and gently from her arms, sensing her grief. She asked when she could see Dustin and was told he would be ready for viewing early on Tuesday. They left the funeral home and went to her mother's house.

Three days had passed and Kim had not been able to see or touch Dustin. She felt so empty. She was hungry, but she could hardly eat. Visiting hours were from 4:00 to 8:00 p.m. that Tuesday. Before visiting hours, Kim patted Dustin on his arms, as his mamma telling him he was going to be all right. She could feel the plastic that he was wrapped in to hold him in one piece.

The officer came to Kim before Dustin was buried and he said "I need to talk to you about your son's crash." This was hard because emotions were high as they were saying their last goodbyes and talking to the hundreds of people that knew and loved Dustin so well.

Visitation could not be held right away because of the necessity of an autopsy, which is done whenever there is a crash. This was labeled a crash and not an 'accident' because law enforcement looks at a crash as an intentional deliberate act that can be prevented. Kim and Danny still didn't know at this point all the details of why they were calling this a 'crash." They greeted about 1,200 people that visited on that Tuesday night. People waited in line for over two hours. It felt to Kim that Dustin was happy to see everyone who came to say goodbye to him. There was a smile on his face in the casket, close to the one in the picture they had given the funeral home.

Danny told people at the funeral "You know he beat me at basketball, running, video games, baseball, and every sport, and now he has beat me to the final resting place. He's in Heaven and I'm not. I know he's smiling about it."

Kim and Danny's hearts were warmed by all the people that came to say goodbye to Dustin. Family, friends, and community were there to support them.

Dustin's Aunt told a story about Dustin at the funeral. One day his Aunt Debby was boating on the Tennessee River in a boat with some people going up the river. She saw this guy on a barn. She said to her husband " I think that guy is going to jump off of that barn." Her husband said " Nah. Nobody is that crazy." As her boat floated by she saw the boy dive into the river from the top of the barn. It scared her. She looked twice, and thought that the boy looked just like Dustin, but concluded that it couldn't be him, so she continued up the river. If she had been sure it was Dustin she would have taken immediate action.

A couple of weeks later she mentioned the incident to Dustin and said, "Dustin, were you over by the Tennessee river a couple of weeks ago?" He said "Yeah I was." She said "Were you on top of a barn?" He said "Yeah I was.." She asked "Was that you jumping into the water?" He said "No, I dove in!" She asked "Do you know how dangerous that was?" He said "Hey. I was impressing the women. I had two blonds with me. I had to make sure they knew I was cool." They learned that yes, it was him after all. At the time all they could do was nervously laugh. The daredevil moment was over. He was all in one piece. But now Aunt Debby recalled mostly how he reflected his love of fun in everything he did.

As they started to leave that night, Serenity was crying, saying that she wanted to get in her Daddy's bed so he could read to her. Her other Grandpa tried to explain that she couldn't do that, even though she kept asking. She didn't understand.

Kim had never known such pain and didn't know her heart could hurt so much. There is a physical pain that comes with the death of a child that cannot be imagined unless you experience it. Serenity's plea brought this pain into focus. Kim's heart ached more than she could ever imagine. It would ache even more once the officer gave them the details of the crash, after everyone had left.

Danny read the autopsy report a month later. He would never let Kim read it. Every bone in Dustin's body, from the neck down, was broken. He had to be wrapped in plastic to keep fluids from seeping out. Kim was concerned that Dustin had suffered, but was assured by many that he did not.

The officer gave them the details leading up to the crash. They were told that a 29-year-old mother named Tiffany Isaza had been partying all day on July 9th (Danny's birthday). She was three times as drunk as the legal limit, with a blood alcohol of .24, and methamphetamine in her system. She had called 911 at 11:30 that night, but hung up the phone. Cleveland police went to Tiffany's Apartment on Blackburn Road in the late hours of the night. She was arguing with her boyfriend, Josh, who allegedly hit her. The police thought that she was a battered woman needing to be rescued. Seeing her bloody lip and bruising and swelling around her left eye, they removed

Josh from the apartment. He pleaded with them, warning them that Tiffany would drive drunk if they left her alone. He continued to plead until the police listened to his plea, and called her mother to come over and make sure Tiffany would not leave her apartment in this state. When the police thought everything was under control, they left the scene of the crime and took Josh with them to the county lock up. Shortly after the police left Tiffany had an argument with her mother and told her to get out of her apartment so her mother left. That was when Tiffany left her two children asleep in bed and drove drunk.

That Friday night Dustin was going 45 miles an hour on APD-40. He was behind another man and had pulled out to pass him. At that moment the man beside him saw the headlights of another car coming toward them, from the wrong direction, at a high rate of speed. He swerved. Then, Dustin tried to swerve and miss the oncoming Ford Taurus, but was unable to. The impact he sustained was that of 120 mph. He did not stand a chance. The engine came in on him and burst his aorta. He was 24 years old. He was an athlete. He was in great physical condition. He worked out every day at The Rush. Nevertheless, he didn't stand a chance because, when a two ton vehicle comes out of nowhere and hits someone unexpectedly as they are coming around a curve, no preventative measures you take ever matter.

The Cleveland City Police remembered Tiffany and the children asleep in their beds. Bradley County deputies returned to the apartment three hours later, early on July 10, after hearing the news of the crash. When they arrived, lights were on and the door was open and unlocked. They found the two children still asleep in separate rooms with no adult present. Tiffany's mother was notified and came to take the children. Josh was released on bond the next day.

Dustin was simply bringing home some eggs and bacon from the Super Walmart, leaving the store at 12:03 a.m. Video footage shows him pushing his cart through the store as he shopped. He could be seen happily talking to the cashier. This was all part of the investigation, which aimed to prove that he was at the Walmart and was indeed driving in the correct direction. He was going the right way on a four lane highway, APD 40, in Bradley County, returning home with the food.

Dustin looked ahead, and out of nowhere headlights beamed straight toward him and a total head on collision occurred at 12:09 a.m. Tiffany Isaza, age 29, was reportedly driving the wrong way on APD-40 between the Overhead Bridge Road and Benton Pike exits. There were nineteen "911" calls reporting that there was a silver Taurus going the wrong way. A "BOLO" (Be On the

Look Out) was immediately initiated by the police. Tiffany L. Isaza, of Cleveland, Tennessee, a mother herself, was intoxicated and was not aware that she was going the wrong way. Dustin was dead, and she was in poor condition in Erlanger hospital, with two broken ankles and a head injury, and did not wake up for two weeks.

Kim lamented the fact she was never going to see her son graduate from college, never see him stand at the altar in the church, watching the love of his life walk down the aisle, never see him celebrate any more birthdays.

The fact that the accident was reportedly due to the other driver being under the influence — someone with children of her own — only compounded the grief. There were days that Kim questioned her faith when she felt like falling apart. But, then she looked at the dew on the daffodils. She remembered how God had met her in her deepest pain before. Little by little, her heartache was healed by God's grace. The pain was still there, but only God could take it and make it meaningful and shine light into this pain. She knew that only God could give a mission to her broken life. There is healing in God's name. Only God could change her weeping and turn it into fighting for justice.

17 A NEW JOURNEY

"No, the heart that has truly loved never forgets, But as truly loves on to the close; As the sunflower turns on her god when he sets; The same look which she turned when he rose."

–Thomas More, *Believe Me*

Kim and Danny dressed for the funeral very slowly. It felt as if every muscle in their bodies ached with grief. Just pulling on the black dress was painful for Kim. Looking in the mirror knowing this was what she was wearing for her son's funeral made it even more real, more final. No words could be said. Tears kept streaming

175

down her cheeks like rain. Danny and Kim were
supported by drivers and hand holders and
prayerful people on the way to the funeral home.
The white pillars out front of the funeral home
looked regal. They drove up to the porte-
cochère and she got out of the car and stepped
into the funeral home. She was not steady on her
feet. She was wearing her fancy high healed dress
shoes to go with this black dress, and was not
accustomed to them. Her grief made her unsteady
as well. Inside, the light yellow walls, white crown
molding, and green carpet were almost cheery. The
funeral director was waiting for them with tissues.
The grandfather clock in the hall ticked quietly.
No one was there yet, but soon the entire chapel
would be filled. Through the window she could
see Pastor Lovelace arriving in his car, a distraught
look on his face. He was a young pastor. Perhaps
he had never ministered to such a tragedy as this
before. The hallway was dotted with golden
framed pictures of those who had long passed, and
Queen Anne chairs, alongside polished end tables
sporting stipple lamps. White flowers that were
carefully placed somehow soothed the top layer of
her grief. She thought for a moment that she could
hold her tears long enough to shake people's hands
in the receiving line. Her family was there to
support her in the side room.

The injustice in this world brought Kim and
Danny down again, but the love they felt for their

son would help them rise up. At first it didn't make sense that God should take Dustin so soon, but God knows what we all need. Life goes on. She told herself that she would press on. She decided to carry on. She felt God hold her closer, and carry her every day with all these burdens on her shoulders, through the deepest pain a woman can know of having lost her child. She knew one day that she was not alone when she felt she knew the purpose of Dustin's death. God gave life to all of creation. It was those same hands that created Dustin, that lifted her up to realize that Dustin's life was not in vain.

Once again Kim and Danny found themselves standing before the face of God to do what is sacred. Tragically, this sacred act was handing their son over to God at the funeral. They were trying to make sense of the senseless tragedy. Their Pastor, Reverend Allan Lovelace, gave a sermon. He spoke of Heaven and how we can only imagine what our eyes will see. Kim's brother-in-law, Gene North, sang out the song, "His strength is perfect when our strength is gone," by Steven Curtis Chapman.

As Gene began to sing, their hearts were touched. It was as if the Lord sang to them and their hearts cried out. Then their neighbor and longtime friend, Lettie, read a tribute to Dustin that touched her heart deeply. She said

"I don't think there was ever a child whose life was more 'celebrated' than Dustin Ledford's. I saw this first-hand as my son Judson Kirkpatrick and Dustin developed a sweet, close friendship through the years as neighborhood and church kids. Kim was a unique 'keeper and creator' of memories in countless ways. I've witnessed it in everything from his amazing home-grown, Halloween costumes, to his elaborate birthday bashes, and even her priceless preservation of his many baseball jerseys into a wonderful blanket. Their lives are filled with 'Dustin' mementos and countless photos. Kim and Danny captured his uniqueness and delighted in it. If ever a child was affirmed and cherished, it was this son that they so clearly knew was a gift from God to their family.

The shortness of his life and the tragedy of his death grieve us all. But the sweetness of his parents' love for him and the memories of how they totally embraced even his brief days will stay with me (and most of those who knew them well) always."

On July 10, 2010 -- the day that Dustin had "succumbed to his injuries in an automobile accident," God called Dustin out into the great unknown as if into oceans deep. When the headlights on that bypass shone in Dustin's face, we are sure Dustin called out God's name to keep his head above it all. At seven years old he asked God to come into his heart and asked Him to forgive his sins. He followed the Lord in Believer's Baptism. He did not always live a perfectly righteous life. But do any of us? Kim knew that sometimes Dustin had fallen into things that he should not have, but this particular event could not have been avoided in any way except by the choices of the reckless driver that fateful night.

While Dustin did not always live his life at the foot of the cross, Kim knew that he believed in God and trusted in Jesus as his personal Savior. In times when she needed comfort she recalled the Bible verses Isaiah 57:1 and 57:2.

"The righteous perish, and no one takes it to heart; The devout are taken away, and no one understands that the righteous are taken away, to be spared from evil. Those who walk uprightly enter into peace; they find rest as they lie in death."

They had no choice but to be still, and let their faith be strengthened. When God called out Dustin's name and he came home to be with God, they had to find a new walk with God. They could not comprehend how God could do this to them; it was so unfair. The depths of their sorrow could not be put into words. Their hearts sank so very deeply. Kim said in prayer "O.K. God. His whole life I've been telling him that you had something special for him. Now what could that be?" And she realized that God does have something special for Dustin. Unfortunately, none of his organs could be salvaged to bring life to others, but still there was more to which his life would be a testimony. Kim knew then that she had to continue living for Dustin.

Even the pastor who was helping Kim through this time did not know that he had ever had to cope with a family in such grief. She cried endlessly. As he prepared to speak at the service for Dustin, he knew that it is good not to internalize grief. The pastor was concerned that Kim was so broken. Members of the congregation were spiritual warriors alongside her the night before the funeral. The prayer chain was called, and people came in shifts. There was not much they could say. "One thing we can be sure of is that God is sovereign," the pastor said. Sometimes things don't make sense to those who are struggling. It was hard to spread the message that God was in control, sovereign over the sudden change, like the storm in the Sea of Galilee in Mark 4:35-41. In that text, a storm came out of nowhere. Jesus said "Be still and believe in the way." It was now time to learn that the storm was not God's will so much as the presence of God to help us get through the storm.

There are no guarantees against the sudden things that come our way. It may be tough to be in a storm with Jesus. The pastor asked everyone to imagine being in a storm without Him. Even when we are people of faith we are transformed, our fear of the flesh from lack of faith makes us cry out. Jesus does hear our cry. In this storm, they turned to Jesus. The pastor assured Kim and Danny that God would assist them in their pain.. The Pastor asked the congregation to consider the feelings of a childless couple. He told of a story of parents who had to choose whether their son would die or be disabled for life. He told of how the mother told the doctor that their child belongs to God, and if God takes him, they are accepting. When he told that story, Kim looked at the pastor and said "We gave him back to God, if he chooses to take him, then we're o.k. We will be o.k." "Yes Kim you're going to be o.k." the pastor said. The Holy Spirit led the pastor in his sermon that day. It was God's way of answering the Pastor's prayer to help the family. Fear and faith compete. He quoted II Timothy 1:7 *"For God hath not given us a spirit of fear, but of power, might, and sound mind."*

We forget that we are still in a fallen world. Faith gets shaky when bad things happen. The Book of James tells us that God can handle our doubts. No one knows why we doubt whether God is able to help us handle our pain and anger. God is. Psalms tell us about these feelings.

After the service in the chapel at the Ralph Buckner Funeral Home, where Pastor Allan Lovelace and Pastor Joe Brooks officiated, it was time to go to Dustin's final resting place. It was hard following the casket in the limousine. Kim knew the pallbearers well, Ben, Blake, Chris, Nick, Andrew, Mikey, Josh and Mike. They were Dustin's cousins, team-mates and friends. She watched as the casket was loaded onto the hearse. The flags were passed out to keep the line of cars together for the procession. As they headed south on Commerce Drive, she looked out the window and held Danny's hand. He put his arm around her. She sobbed onto the lapel of his jacket. The green trees and fields they passed on the way flickered by like light. Soon they were there at the top of Sunset Memorial Gardens. It was only a fifteen-minute drive. They had selected this particular cemetery because Kim's daddy was buried there, and where her mom would one day be buried. . Kim's sister owned lots there, too, and Danny's dad and mom were buried there. Danny and Kim had bought lots there 21 years ago. They still have two lots left for themselves to rest next to Dustin. They liked it because it overlooked Cleveland's beautiful sunsets from the top of the hill.

They had a short service in the hot sun that Wednesday afternoon. The white doves were released and they flew high into the blue sky on that hot summer day. The sun beat down on their black clothes and the heat made their suits and ties and black dresses as unbearable as their grief. They lowered the casket, and placed a rose on it. Dirt was shoveled over Dustin as he was laid to rest. Somberly, everyone left in their cars to drive home and go on with their lives. At that moment it felt like their lives had stopped.

Weeks after the funeral Kim and Danny were still struck with grief. Kim knew that she had to share Dustin's story with others. She hoped that people would remember to make the right choice not to drink and drive. Then she heard a still small voice speak to her. Her strong will knew something in this world had to change and maybe it could be her voice that could make that happen. If not now, then when could she be part of the change she wanted to see? If not her, then who would speak out? Kim and Danny felt moved to do something to make sense out of their tragic loss. She realized that God wanted her to do something and that He put her in this position because He knew she could carry this burden. She heard His voice call her name to bring her pain and her sorrow to him and go out into the world and change it so car crashes caused by drunk drivers would not kill others. Once again she prayed to God. She brought Him her doubts and fears, her hurt and her tears. She listened to the guidance to wait upon the Lord. Her heart yearned to cry tears of joy someday. She knew this would take time. She did not want to be shaken by this to the point of turning away from God.

The next day they got a call from MADD, Mothers Against Drunk Drivers, an organization that supports victims of drunk drivers, asking if they could be of support in any way. They reached out to both Danny and Kim and came to court with them. Julie Strike went with them every step of the way through the judicial process. Kim and Danny were so grateful for their support. Only a victim could truly understand their pain. Julie had been in an accident herself that was caused by a drunk driver. From personal experience she knew the injustice of accidents caused by drunk drivers. Julie Strike sat with them in court as they waited for the judge's verdict. Julie told Kim how moved she was to hear how hard it was for Danny. All the people who wrote letters on their behalf, all the honesty, support from friends, organizations, and family, and personal prayer helped to get them to overcome some of their grief. Kim learned how to take her pain and use it for a purpose. She grew as a person and as a speaker. Through M.A.D.D. she found refuge. Her hope was in the Lord that led her to crusade to protect others from such a fate and to persuade others to make better choices.

Every day as Danny and Kim awoke, and the sun rose up on the hills of Cleveland, Tennessee, there was an empty place in their hearts. There was an empty place at their table. The one who was supposed to live on past them was gone. The one they had planned to pass the torch when they passed on was no longer in the race. They had just grown strong enough to move back to their home. A new sense of normal had just set in, but it was not really normal. Just as they had started a new routine, the news of the trial to judge Tiffany Isaza for the crimes she was arrested of vehicular homicide by intoxication and child neglect. They marked the date on the calendar and planned to attend. Kim was shaking all through the trial. She did not know how she could get through hearing the whole story again. Julie Strike from MADD and the Victim Impact Panel came with her and held her hand through the proceedings. Having a compassionate witness present gave her strength. Just hearing that original story from the officer retold was almost unbearable. Danny sat on her other side and they got through it together. Tiffany was charged with vehicular homicide and was given a ten-year sentence. At the end of the trial, Kim was given some names that she numbly wrote down, not fully able to process the impact of all that was said that day.

The District Attorney informed her that the Board of Parole provided services to crime victims, and that in the future she may need to navigate the parole process. As a crime victim, she had the right to be notified of the parole hearings involving Tiffany Isaza, once she registered with the Board of Parole. He kindly explained that she could complete a victim impact statement with the Board.

Kim went home and sank into her quiet space of prayer. Days later she drafted her victim's impact statement that would become a part of Tiffany's file, and one day reviewed by Parole Board members. This would be ready if ever Tiffany became eligible for parole consideration. She did not think that would be soon, but she did it anyway. In time, Victim Services gave her information on the parole process, and would accompany her at the parole hearings for support.

Kim was grateful she lived in Tennessee. Not all states gave victims these legal rights. They respected her and had compassion for her broken heart. Kim survived this crime and through hard work was able to insure her voice was heard, valued, and included in a collective effort to hold Tiffany accountable. She collected signatures, petitions, and asked people to write letters on her behalf. It was her hope that she could prevent Tiffany from inflicting future harm on others. It was also her hope that others could be discouraged from drinking and driving. She realized more needed to be done. Penalties needed to be harsher for vehicular homicide.

Convincing the Board required more than just her voice. It required community support. Kim got that support and her voice was heard throughout the halls of Congress. It was heard beyond the walls of the parole hearing. In fact Representative Eric Watson of Tennessee heard her voice and wanted her to speak before the Legislature to get tougher drunk driving laws passed.

And so they chose to create something in Dustin's honor that would live on past them. Dustin changed their world with his love and laughter. They thought his love would change the world. It did, but just not in the way that they had thought it would.

Danny and Kim worked diligently to make the justice system work on their behalf. Representative Dan Howell reached out to them when he was trying to pass House Bill 457, to make the penalties for drunk drivers stiffer. They went to hearings, and spoke out about the need for the criminal justice system to make sure people who recklessly drive are severely penalized. Senator Gardenhire sponsored Senate Bill 454 to do the same. These legislators were working tirelessly for their constituency and wanted to make positive change to detour others from making the same mistake as Tiffany. Whenever Kim was asked to speak on the need for this law, she was there.

This bill changes the definition of a Class A felony offense of aggravated vehicular homicide to anyone with a blood alcohol level of 0.20 or more; or a blood alcohol content of 0.08 percent or more and any blood concentration of methamphetamine.

Tiffany made a choice to start that car. Tiffany made a choice to put it in reverse, and back out and go the wrong way on a one way highway. Because of her choice, Danny and Kim had to choose a casket, cemetery plot, a final set of clothes, and funeral arrangements for their child. They worked tirelessly to make sure Isaza served her sentence. Tiffany's choice took away many of their future life choices. Kim and Danny were instrumental in forming scholarships that were funded by the golf tournament that is held annually at Chatata Valley Golf Course in Cleveland. The name of the tournament is the Dustin Ledford "Live Wide Open" Golf Tournament. This is an annual event in the community now. Danny and Kim have made a positive influence in the lives of the individuals who really listen to their talks for the Mothers Against Drunk Driving Organization and the Victim's Impact Panel.

The Dustin Ledford Scholarship is designed to reward an average, hardworking, athletic college-bound senior, with the goal of helping young athletes who show promise. In order to be eligible for this scholarship they have to write an essay on the dangers of drinking and driving. This scholarship includes all sports, including cheerleading, and is a one-time award of $1,000.00 for a senior entering college. It goes to all three of the area high schools. Since its inception they have given over $20,000.00 to benefit over 15 or more students. Their goal of making the world better in Dustin's name brings their heart back into their lives. It provides solace, knowing that the funds raised in Dustin's name will bring awareness to their cause and will help others.

Dustin would like that. He, too, was once a student going to college. He was a 2004 graduate of Bradley High School who was much loved by his peers and played baseball for Bradley. Dustin would have been pleased to know that others will read his life story and will want to make a difference by speaking out.

God was moving in their lives. It felt as if this was His plan all along, and was welcomed into their hearts. Previously, everything Kim could give was always given to her husband and Dustin. Similarly, Danny had focused his life on making them both happy.

Now Danny worried that Kim would never be happy again. He would move heaven and earth to see a smile on his bride again. Now everything was changed overnight and they had to look to their God who was unchangeable to guide them. Danny grieved just as she did. He also supported Kim in her grieving process.

God guided Kim to give of herself and time. When she first walked into a group of people ready to listen to her story, she felt the presence of

Dustin and love bursting inside, as it always had, but in a new way. She felt a passion to explain to young people in colleges, universities, and schools that making just one bad choice can kill people. This passion burned strongly in her heart. They spread a seed to make others recognize that, hasty, thoughtless choices we make can end up being murder. Each of us needs to be mindful and watchful. Kim's passion to explain burned like wildfire. The light of the Lord blessed her to do good in the world on behalf of her son. Now Dustin's life had meaning for her.

In Danny and Kim's desperation, God's foundation would get them through the torment they felt. Their marriage was a marriage given to God. God got them through this. Their love did too.

Kim realized that Danny and she would never put 25 candles on a birthday cake for Dustin. Every Mother's Day, she is torn between joy and sorrow. Joy, because she enjoyed almost 25 years of being the mother of Dustin sorrow, because Dustin is gone. Now Danny's birthday is the anniversary of their son's death. Danny's birthday celebration for years to come will never be the same. Dustin was a son, a grandson, a cousin, a fiancé, and a father to Serenity, the daughter of his fiancée. Instead of shopping for gifts for her son, Kim has had to buy flowers for his grave.

Danny is grateful for the chance to have been Dustin's teacher. Kim and Danny have endured this experience of losing a child together. They say the chances of a marriage breaking up within a year of losing a child are very high, but Danny can think of no one else he would rather share this experience with than his wife. She and Danny are one another's rock. If she has a bad day, he's o.k. If he has a bad day, she's o.k. He doesn't know what they will do if they ever have a bad day at the same time!

Kim misses the times when Dustin used to call and say "Hey Mom, what are you doing?" or "Love you, Mom," or "Happy Mother's Day — I love you." You are called a widow or widower when you lose your spouse. You are called an orphan when you lose your parents. You have no word for when you lose a child. You are left alone in the dark with an absence more powerful than any. The past washes up onto the shores of your heart with sweet memories. That is all you have left.

For Kim and Danny, the future seemed unimaginable at first. Then there were those with compassion who showed them little paths forward that few have had to tread. It was as if they were standing at the shore and they knew it was time to resume their lives, but they couldn't go back to how it used to be. They had to make a new way in the sand. Little guideposts along the way led them.

They picked themselves up and they went on because they knew there must be a reason.

The MADD organization gave Dustin's parents a path to move forward and give meaning to their loss. This path takes time. There are days when they stumble and fall and continue to grieve, but they go on because they can hear the distant waves washing upon their heart again with sea foam memories. They have dedicated themselves to teaching others about the consequences of bad decisions when behind the wheel. They speak regularly to tell their story. So much of their past life was about making the right choices. They had learned to forgive, live on, love on, and forget misgivings and bad guidance in the past. So there came a time to stand up and try to stop any further nonsense.

A new beginning arose from the ashes of this loss. They had bracelets created that say "D-Led" on them, because that is what Dustin called himself on the baseball team. It wasn't Dustin Ledford; it was "D-Led." It also has his date of death, 7/10/2010. It has II Timothy 1:7, his favorite Bible verse that he learned at age eight in Vacation Bible School, and it says *"God has not given us a spirit and fear but of power and might so that we may have a sound mind."* And it has three little words: "Live Wide Open!" because Dustin Ledford lived life wide open. It is Kim and Danny's hope that people take this bracelet and wear it or hang it on their rear view mirror. Maybe the bracelet will spark something inside of those who are on the brink of making a life-changing decision to think of getting a designated driver, or to just slow down. Kim is honored each time someone takes a bracelet home with them from one of her talks.

Kim and Danny spoke at Dustin's trial and came back for Tiffany's parole hearing. Tiffany was then required to continue serving her sentence. Hundreds of letters opposing Tiffany's possible parole had been sent to the Parole Board, which warmed their hearts. While it did not make the pain go away, it helped them know that there were people that cared for justice.

Danny and Kim kept their hearts open

to their memories and shared them with the world. More letters, along with a petition with more than a thousand signatures, poured into their mailbox. At least Dustin's death was not pointless. Kim and Danny are boldly living their life sentence of a son gone from their future. They walk that path with their heads held high. They walk that path reaching out to others who will listen or care.

18 JUSTICE

"There is no debt with so much prejudice put off as that of justice."
    —Plutarch

About eighteen months after the trial, Kim received a letter from the Parole Board, informing her of the time and date of Tiffany's parole hearing in September. She could not believe the words. It was too soon for Tiffany to get a chance to be free.

Kim's heart sank, but she had time to prepare and she was ready. They had already traveled all over the state sharing their story -- in Tennessee, Florida, Ohio, Indiana, Georgia, and anywhere where there was an audience. But it was a blow to think of the possibility of Tiffany getting time off for good behavior and being considered for parole.

Some days when Kim and Danny are in the routine of their daily life, they momentarily forget that Dustin is gone. The day the letter came was not one of those days. When Kim cooked Dustin's favorite chicken casserole, she remembered. If the bottles of tears they cried lined the shelf in her pantry, there would be no room for food there but still they go on and live their lives. When the table is set, that empty space is still there, but, there is a new place for petitions, paperwork, and planning strategies to keep drunk drivers off the road.

Kim was ready to share her grieving words, petitions and planning. Her ability to speak had taken them everywhere. Now it was time to go to the Women's Penitentiary in Nashville. There they testified about their son's death in hopes of keeping Tiffany, the woman convicted of killing him, in prison. Kim and Danny were sitting in the room with the woman who killed their son by her reckless actions. Tiffany Isaza had spent two years of a ten-year sentence, and the Parole Board was considering releasing her early for good behavior, even though Tiffany took no responsibility for her transgressions. But then Kim spoke and delivered her petitions, and letters.

They were reminded how Tiffany was sentenced originally to eight years in the Tennessee Department of Corrections, as well as two years on child endangerment, because she left her children alone to go out. The poor children lost their mother the night of the tragic crash. Like most addicts, Tiffany was able to rationalize her behavior. While driving drunk, her spatial reasoning declined, she felt in control, powerful, confident. Kim spoke of all the details of the horrible crash, and of Dustin's innocent drive that ended in his death.

The District Attorney's Office heard Kim and Danny's story. They were equally appalled by Tiffany's possibility of parole. The Assistant District Attorney, Brooklyn Martin Townsend, helped the 10th Judicial District Attorney General's Office prepare a letter in opposition to Tiffany's possibility of parole. They wanted her to serve the full ten-year sentence. They believed a just system should value the voice of the victims. They believed that Dustin's family should have a chance to voice their opposition to early parole.

Kim and Danny's voices were heard loud and clear. They spoke of choices. If we are to live in a society together as human beings we must be responsible and held accountable for our choices. Tiffany Isaza made a "choice" that night to get behind the wheel of a car even though she was impaired. Kim and Danny let it be known how that choice changed their lives. They understand how people make bad choices every day, but they also believe in accountability. How else can Tiffany be accountable for her actions? Our judicial system needs to bring forth accountability. This is what brings about change.

Kim and Danny had spent too many years walking on their new journey without their precious son -- 26 months of a life sentence. Tiffany had spent only 22 months in jail of a 10-year sentence. Those 26 months translate to 788 days without seeing or holding Dustin, missing his 25th and 26th birthdays, two Halloweens, two Thanksgivings, two Christmases, two Valentine's Days, two of their birthdays, two Mother's Days, and two Father's Days. A person's life is surely worth more than a mere 22 months of incarceration.

Memories of Dustin's first steps, his first tooth, his first trip to Disney World, his high school proms, every birthday and Christmas, the way his eyes lit up when Santa came, are all Kim and Danny have of Dustin now. They treasure these memories. They remind us all to keep our faith in God and treasure our loved ones now.

When Dustin was first born, Kim saved a poem from the newspaper in a memorabilia box. Four months after he died, she was going through that box to revisit memories, when she found this poem she read it again.

To all parents......

I'll lend you, a little while,
A child of mine, He said.
For you to love while he lives,
And mourn when he is dead.
It may be six or seven years,
Or twenty-two or three.
But will you, till I call him back,
Take care of him for Me?
He'll bring his charms to gladden you,
And shall his stay be brief.
You'll have his lovely memories,
As solace for your grief.
I cannot promise he will stay,
As all from earth return.
But there are lessons taught down there,
I want this child to learn.
I've looked the wide world over,
In my search for teachers true.
And from the throngs that crowd life's lanes,
I have selected you.
Now will you give him all your love,

Not think the labour vain.
Nor hate me when I come to call
To take him home again?
I fancied that I heard them say,
'Dear Lord, Thy will be done!'
For all the joys this child shall bring,
The risk of grief we'll run.
We'll shower him with tenderness,
And love him while we may,
And for the happiness we've known,
Forever grateful stay.
And should the angels call for him,
Much sooner than we planned.
We'll brave the bitter grief that comes,
And try to understand.

'A Child Of Mine'   -by Edgar Guest

In Danny's eyes, Dustin was an ugly little baby who grew up to be such a handsome young man. Every person who comes into this world is a living, vibrant being who will write their story onto the face of this earth. Each of us leave footprints on the path we walk. Sometimes those footprints are washed away by the waves of time. Sometimes people follow the same path and learn by tracing where those feet have trod. Each life is like a book written by God. We know the author of our happenstance. Philosophers question whether or not God himself wrote our life story we were predestined to live before we were born, or if our lives happen out of the choices we make. Either way, we each have a life story that has a beginning, middle, and end just as a book does. When the book is slammed shut, and no more pages can be turned, and the music has stopped unnaturally, it is a shock. We futilely hope there must be something we can do to change the ending of a life so close to us. There would be if it was a book we could write ourselves. Time after time we are reminded the true author of our story is more elusive. It is a script that can be silenced by forces beyond our control. For parents, it is the hardest silence to face. It is hard to accept that the book they had been intending to read into their older years has been shut, never to be opened again. The corner of the last page often curls up just a bit, tempting them with what might have been. That page, however, is held down by a force beyond their control.

Each one of us has a completely unique story set to unfold. Some are born into fabulously rich families while others are born into wretchedly poor families. One child may be born as handsome, while another is born deformed or unsightly. Some babies are born healthy and strong, while others are born weak and handicapped. Why do such disparities exist?

As a parent, you mistakenly think you are master of this little life that you have watched grow into young adulthood. When their story stays untold, their song is left unsung, it can feel like being lost in an alternate universe. No longer can you wait for the dreams you had for your child's life. To accept that nothing will unfold, that nothing will ever bring back the fruit of your parenting, is torture.

Many parents have conversations with God about how their child's life will unfold. They worry, they feel responsible. What do the wise men and sages say about this? Do we have free will? One view is that everything is predestined and that we have no influence. It seems unthinkable that Dustin's fate was sealed and he was destined to die so young. The other view is that we do have control and we are completely free to mold and shape the world and our children's lives as we see best. Perhaps neither of these positions is true. Bad things do happen to good people.

The control we have on our lives and those of our children is limited. For example, imagine a cow tied to a rope that is pegged to the ground. We know this cow can move about in a circle in a radius equal to the length of the rope. This rope has a "sphere of influence," and likewise, so do parents. When the cow is moving around in that circle, the cow will not even feel the presence of the rope. When the cow tries to move beyond the circle, immediately the rope pulls it back. When parents want to exert influence to change a life, it is futile when there are forces beyond their control -- this is the situation as a parent.

There is a circle in which we can freely move around and make choices about our own lives and how we influence the lives of our children. Our free will rests within the radius of that circle. Beyond that tether we must give up to God because there is nothing we can do. As the serenity prayer says, "God grant me the courage to change the things I can, the serenity to accept the things I cannot change, and the wisdom to know the difference."

Every choice we make can be made through devotion to God with our will, or with our reaction to the will of others. You can be awakened by an alarm clock, but you still need willpower to get up. If you use willpower, then you are motivated by your own will, which is empowering and energizing. Dustin lived that way. He had the will to move forward in all he did. He did not do what he "had" to do. He did what he wanted to do.

Dustin lived his life with passion, with power, and with might. Kim and Danny carried on because they were going to abide by Dustin's verse "God hath not given us a spirit of fear, but of power and might." This one verse helped them realize that God was with them every step of their painful journey to help them face everything. They were not going to give in to confusion, depression, and hopelessness, from then, on. They knew that Dustin's life had planted a tree of power and might in their lives that would continue on. There was no seed of fear to grow negative fruits. There were days of pain and sorrow, but they chose to live their lives in power and might.

There was nothing that Kim and Danny could have done that fateful night. The circle of influence that had crossed Dustin's life was Tiffany's. Her radius of influence was small, she thought, and so she behaved in small ways. We are each tethered to our own center force. The ways in which we order our lives overlap onto the lives of others. The small choices we make can make big changes for others.

There are rules in the game of life. There are consequences for the things that we do. These consequences are inevitable. This law is impersonal. Tiffany thought she could overlook the laws of nature and her actions would show no consequences. The laws of "Cause and Effect" are recognized in all walks of life. What we do is the basis of what we are. What we are doing now is the basis of what we will be.

It is easy to be discouraged when you think about what happened to Dustin and how unfair it was that such a positive, powerful young man would be cut down in the prime of his life. It is easy to fall into the trap of fear about the tragedy in the world. But his verse tells us not to fear. God has not given us a spirit of fear. God gave us a spirit of love, power and sound mind. Dustin spoke and lived by this verse. It was the legacy he left. We have the power to make choices. We have the power to make loving choices and act in loving ways. God's power is backing our work. The spirit of Love works through us in all we do when we are close to God and do things as God would want us to do. He gives us a sound mind to discern right from wrong.

19. A FEARLESS INVENTORY

There are some things which men[and women] confess with ease, and others with difficulty.

–Epictetus,

Kim has made a searching and fearless inventory of herself as she developed the speeches she made for the Mothers Against Drunk Driving organization. She knew she should never have become pregnant when she was sixteen. She now admits she was rebellious. It took courage to give up her child to a good home with a good family that could raise that new life to be the best that she could be. She had decided to trust the Lord. She turned her will and her life over to God's care. Her willingness to trust God was called upon many times. She had to trust God when she had the hysterectomy. She had to accept her path to motherhood and take on that responsibility seriously.

Telling her story about Dustin helps Kim accept the new inventory of her life. She always looks forward. Just three weeks after the accident,

Kim went to Tiffany and told her she forgave her. She did not do that for Tiffany. She did it so that her own heart would not be hardened. She did not want that root of bitterness to grow within her. It still is an ongoing process. Every morning when she wakes up and her child is not there, she has to continually ask God to help her forgive. Every day Dustin is gone she is surveying or examining thoughts, events, emotions, and actions in her life and thinking about what led her to be his mother. When she completes her inventory, it includes every day she was with Dustin and she is grateful for that.

Months after the first parole hearing, Kim received several letters from Tiffany explaining why she drove drunk and high and killed her son. Kim was stunned. Tiffany never took responsibility for her actions. She read a laundry list of blame and excuses. She has written four or five letters. In her first letter, Tiffany blamed the alcohol use on a "witchdoctor that put a voodoo curse on her" which made her drink. In her second letter, she blamed her upbringing in an abusive home for her drinking. All Kim wanted to hear from her was that she accepted responsibility for her actions that night. She truly hopes that Tiffany does change her life when she gets out of prison, and can make something good come from this so that Dustin did not die in vain.

Being fearless and honest about how you got

to this point in your life is not easy. Kim knew this. Kim knew Tiffany had much to fear. She did not ask her to not be afraid. Tiffany persistently refused to look at her actions to admit where she made choices in her life that killed Kim's son. She understood Tiffany must have experienced many emotions as she surveyed what she did. The letters made Kim wonder if Tiffany felt embarrassment or shame or fear which was preventing her from owning the blame.

For if Tiffany were to make a fearless inventory of herself it would probably be overwhelming, as it would be for anyone recovering from addiction. Many who struggle with addiction stop at this step and are unwilling to make this inventory. "Without a searching and fearless moral inventory, the faith which really works in daily living is still out of reach." (Twelve Steps and Twelve Traditions, 1981, 43).

While Kim is confident each of us has our own walk with God, whether we want to claim a God or not, she wants Tiffany to claim responsibility for what she did. While she has behaved well in prison, she likely could slip into the same addictive behaviors that originally led to that fateful night. The evidence is plain that she had a substance abuse problem. There is a twelve step program in the prison system. Perhaps she participated in it or perhasps she still thinks she does not have a substance abuse problem or that she does not have the power to change. This is just a first step to help heal the wounds she inflicted on Dustin and his family. In discovering her own destructive tendencies, she could take the first step toward correcting them. This is difficult, but it could enable her to better understand Kim's pain. It is this kind of faith and hope Tiffany will need if she is to continue her recovery and overcome her addiction. Self-honesty about your role in your own addiction is part of any substance abuse program.

Many addicts are known to just go through the motions and say what needs to be said just to get through their program. They show up to AA meetings, sign their name, and leave. These people do not stay in recovery. An inventory is a very personal process, and there is no single right way to do it. Those who have already done an inventory realize that you need to be honest with yourself and seek the Lord's guidance or your own personal power.

It is hoped that Tiffany could be truthful and loving as she sorts through her memories and feelings. *"(People) will continue with (their) original addiction or switch to another one. Their addiction is a symptom of other causes and conditions."*(Alcoholism, Keith Humphreys* and Rudolf Moos. 2001, 64).

At first Tiffany was able to look at the incident, and give a short description of her memory of the event, in summary form. While she could explain the effect on herself, she could not entirely grasp the effect on anyone else. Tiffany's unchanged feelings in the letters Kim received about the incident were of self-indulgence and self-pity. Tiffany's attempts at self-examination failed to acknowledge how her character weaknesses or strengths affected the situation. Kim knows that at times Tiffany may have acted right, and prays that lessons have been learned and that she will never repeat her former mistakes.

All of us need to humble ourselves at some time in our lives -- perhaps later in life with a failed marriage, a job or business loss, an illness, or a bankruptcy. This is a time when we need to face the painful truth about ourselves and our actions.

This painful process of seeing our true selves keeps us humble and realistic, and helps to prevent our repeating our mistakes. For Kim, it was when she recognized her part in becoming pregnant, and recognized her own weaknesses. Nevertheless, she had the strength to do the responsible thing by give child for adoption to a good Christian home. This opened her heart to and be an adoptive mother to another baby that was given to her. A power greater than she helped her recognize her strength to carry on. She and Danny chose to live the life that God had planned for them. Danny is also a hero in this story for being strong throughout the storms they weathered together with God as an anchor.

Kim and Danny hope that Tiffany might be able to look at herself in the mirror and face her addictions. Alcoholics Anonymous would probably encourage her to ask herself questions like:

What outcome did I want when I chose to leave my children and drive drunk? Why?

Would I have done it again if I had not gotten caught?

Would I do it now for another drink?

How did I try to control my need for another drink?

Why did I get in that car and go to the convenience store?

What actions did I take to get what I wanted?

How could I ignore the reality that I was already drunk and should not have been driving?

Was it reasonable to think I could drive drunk and leave my children alone? Why not?

How did I lie to myself or to others?

How did I ignore the feelings of others and think only of myself? Have I considered the feelings of the victims of my crime?

How did I act like a victim to control others, get attention and sympathy, be special, and so on?

Did I resist help from God and others?

Did I insist on being right?

Did I feel slighted for lack of recognition or acknowledgment?

Kim and Danny are forever grateful for the inspired counsel they received in their time of need. There was support from so many unexpected places. They attended a grief class that encouraged them to share their troubling feelings. Friends came and held their hands, brought meals, and listened. Family was always there to lift them up when they needed it. Their faith in the Lord gave them comfort. Daily prayer and contemplation were major factors in their recovery from grief. They stood side by side and held each other's hands. Their love for one another sustained them, too. They turned to God for comfort, courage, and guidance. They found the help that continues with them to this day. Paul taught that God is the "God of all comfort; who comforteth us in all our tribulation." (II Corinthians 1:3-4). God will help you each time sit with grief you and pray. God was always there for them. And, perhaps one day Tiffany will turn to God, and God will be there waiting.

While Kim has forgiven Tiffany, a place of

reconciliation has not yet been forged. Maybe with prayer and time, they will be able to come to an understanding and acceptance. Soon Tiffany will be eligible for parole, and Kim will not go to her final parole hearing to speak on behalf of lengthening her sentence, but to accept her parole. It was so stressful the last time she went to the parole hearing. The realization that Tiffany's children paid the price of this sentence, weighed heavily on Kim's heart. She is ready to take justice away from its narrow adversarial focus and understand instead that it much more strongly refers to the obligation to be fair, and maybe even leave room for healing in the community. She knows the time Tiffany has served behind bars made a difference in the lives of many. Perhaps more people will think twice before they drink and drive now. Perhaps she saved others from being victimized by Tiffany's carelessness again. Perhaps Tiffany will now understand there are consequences for her actions, and not repeat her crime. Kim will never restore her life to the way it was before Dustin died, but she is now opening her heart to a place which doesn't ask how we can punish Tiffany but rather how we can find an inner peace which accepts that we are all human beings and that we are not separate even from those who have hurt us. It is time to close this story's focus on Tiffany's punishment and move toward reconciliation. Hopefully Tiffany will prove to society that she can be a better person.

2O HOPE

"Beyond this vale of tears, There is a life above, unmeasured by the flight of years, And all that life is love."

– James Montgomery

There are so many paths a life can take. No one's life should be lived in vain. What legacy we leave is not only ours to choose. We do not know the reason for our existence in the larger scheme of things. The reasons will unfold in due time.

In 2014, Kim was awarded the Voice for Victims Award. She helped plant a tree at a victim memorial site. She has been recognized for her talent in speaking out. She will continue to speak for the rights of ordinary citizens to be safe. Kim is not drowning in her sorrow. She knows that despite laws and MADD, drunk driving deaths will still happen, but she's working to help people use proper judgment before driving, especially if there are distractions that could make their car a deadly weapon. She wants people to think twice about the consequences of their actions. She has a mother's mandate to act, and has been on a mission to turn tragedy into something good. She does not want another parent to have to bury their child because of a reckless, intoxicated driver. God has given her the ability to advocate for this cause. She believes God is using her to deliver this message from Dustin.

Letter-writing campaigns were forged in Dustin's name. Kim continued to speak out. Newspaper articles were written on Dustin's behalf. Kim and Danny collaborated with Tennessee lawmakers to seek tougher DUI punishments. They went to Nashville to testify to local lawmakers. In February of 2014, they gathered again with other families of victims to keep pushing for legislation to boost penalties for those that kill others due to their intoxication and reckless driving.

Kim and Danny have spoken at several schools about the dangers of driving under the influence of drugs or alcohol. As mentioned earlier, Kim also worked with State Representative Eric Watson who is now Sheriff in Bradley County to have "Dustin's Law" (Senate SB0454, and the House HB0457) passed in Tennessee. The bill has already passed in the House and the Senate due to the work of Honorable Representatives Kevin Brooks, Dan Howell, and Honorable Senators Todd Gardenhire, and Mike Bell who authored it. It will not be made law until it can be approved by the Finance Committee. Funding is the major obstacle. The State of Tennessee needed about $445,000 to pay for the extra incarceration. Unfortunately, Rep. Eric Watson, (R-Cleveland), Sen. Todd Gardenhire, (R-Chattanooga), Senator Mike Bell,(R-Riceville), Rep. Kevin Brooks (R-Cleveland) Rep Dan Howell (R-Cleveland) and the families were unable to persuade Governor Bill Haslam and his legislative colleagues to find enough money in their budget yet to pay for "Dustin's Law." The work of Senator Todd Gardenhire gave Kim and Danny solace that there are still legislators that honestly and faithfully listen to the needs of their constituency.

Representative Watson and Senator Gardenhire met Kim and Danny at the State Capitol news conference to speak out and make positive social change. Kim couldn't help but think Dustin would be proud to have the Bill named after him and Kim hoped it would become law.

They wanted to redefine aggravated vehicular homicide so it would be classified as a Class A felony. The definition would include a driver with a blood alcohol content (BAC) of .20 or a BAC of .08 and methamphetamine in their system. Currently, a conviction of aggravated vehicular homicide is given if the defendant commits vehicular homicide and has two or more previous convictions for DUI, a previous conviction for vehicular homicide, vehicular assault, or any combination of the two.

If Senators Gardenhire, and Bell and Representatives Brooks and Howell are able to get the Bill passed, the current penalties from 8 to 12 years imprisonment would increase to 16 to 20 years. Rep. William Lamberth, (R-Portland), a former Assistant Prosecutor, said that in some cases, offenders could be sentenced to as much as 60 years.

Coming together with other parents in the State Capitol news conference room showed Kim and Danny that they were not alone. When they spoke at the news conference, they were accompanied by Susan Pagan, whose 13-year-old daughter, Ciara Alexis Pagan, was killed in a single-car accident in Cleveland in September in 2013. It was equally sad for her to learn that Ciara's friend's father was drunk at the time he was driving children to a local skating rink. Even though he was charged with vehicular homicide and two counts of reckless endangerment, the consequences for his actions are suffered more by the victims than the perpetrator. Kim and Danny tried to console Susan Pagan. When they talked to her, her voice wavered as she clutched her daughter's teddy bear. She had lost her child under the same circumstances.

It is time for the people of Tennessee to have legislation that requires individuals to take responsibility for their actions. Many other states have more rigorous legislation. For example, as of 2012, all fifty states have laws permitting the installation of ignition-interlock devices as sentencing alternatives for drunken drivers. Ten states make it mandatory for drunk drivers to blow into a breathalyzer before their car will start. If the police had been able to attach that to Tiffany's car that night, Dustin's life would have been saved.

Money was all it would take to pass and implement this law, but unfortunately, the legislators in the Finance Committee were unable to come up with this money. Danny and Kim are still trying to get the bill passed. Some legislators have been working tirelessly to create laws in Tennessee that protect the people from drunk drivers.

Kim and Danny's tireless voices have woken up Tennessee and the state is now ready to consider ways to make roads safer for all of their citizens. More legislation has been passed and made into law. HB013 and SB0456 have been enacted to require the use of transdermal monitoring on persons previously charged with vehicular homicide who have prior alcohol-related motor vehicle convictions. Also it creates an offense to tamper with or remove a monitoring device.

According to the U.S. Department of Justice, Office of Justice Programs, "Although alcohol consumption and alcohol-related deaths are in decline, alcohol abuse is still linked to a large percentage of criminal offenses." Statistics (Bureau of Justice Statistics) show that almost four in ten violent crimes involve alcohol, according to the crime victim, as do four in ten fatal motor vehicle accidents. And about four in ten criminal offenders report that they were using alcohol at the time of their offense.

Dustin was just one of the 13,365 deaths in 2010 caused by a drunk driver. The one in five victims who were lucky enough to come out of an alcohol-related violent incident alive (about 500,000 victims annually) suffered losses totaling more than $400 million. When injured in alcohol-related violence, the average victim experienced a $1,500 out-of-pocket medical expense.

Legislators with compassion for their constituency have looked at the financial loss alcohol related crimes causes victims. Rather than simply pass on the costs to the victims these new measures pass the costs on to the perpetrators.

The numbers of deaths have gone down a bit recently. Perhaps it is the awareness in the community that is being forged. But the battle against this problem is still not won. According to MADD (Mothers Against Drunk Driving), 277 people died in the state of Tennessee in 2013 as the result of drunk drivers. In 2010 all across the United States there were 10, 637 DUI caused fatalities. 248 of those were in Tennessee. Dustin was one of those 248. How much should it cost to stop these people? How much are these lives worth? If these legislators think $445,000 is too much money, we must ask how much is enough? How much would it cost to stop these people? If we put a price on these lives we are only asking for $1606.49 per death. The individual lives lost are worth far more than $1606.49 each. If a Bill proposed that the money come from the pockets of the perpetrators, perhaps this could fund prevention   measures.

If Kim's efforts stop one or two people from

making the wrong choice to drink and drive, she will know her work has been for a reason worthwhile. The t-shirts with Dustin's photo on the front and on the back, the words: "Killed by a drunk driver and I'm MADD" send a message to others every day. Every time someone looks at one of these t-shirts being sold to raise funds to support the MADD campaign, there will be a message in the back of their mind not to drink and drive. Every time the community sees scores of people walking together to support efforts against drunk driving they will see Danny and Kim walking side by side with that group and they will know it is a powerful way they have been able to walk forward in their lives. They chose to walk forward in their lives because they know their story might save others from a fate as theirs.

Kim and Danny share this story in hopes they can save one person from making the wrong choice, so that Dustin's life was not insignificant. Kim encourages public support of her message. They forgive Tiffany but believe it is best for her to serve her time. They are consoled by their vision of heaven. Kim and Danny have a dream of the afterlife where they will be with Dustin. They know that their beloved Father knows -- even now, since Dustin's passing -- how deeply they loved and missed him.

Kim and Danny know that when they die, they will once again be able to talk to their beloved son. Once again there will be three sets of footprints in the sand. In that vision they have crossed over and look up at him and see that he recognizes them. He is standing on the other side in Heaven with the Lord. They will share the moments they wished they could have shared with him on earth after his passing and all their sense of loss will be healed. All the lonely holidays, and birthdays will not matter anymore. In that dream of the sweet 'by and by,' they envision a time when they will meet again, in heaven and remember who and what they were to each other. A mother will embrace her son, and a father his will embrace his son. When they leave this dream and live in the present their pain still radiates powerfully through their heartfelt dreams. The reality that he is no longer in sharing days with them stings their hearts. They are spiritually linked to Dustin, having lived life through him for so long.

Now what remains to be done is charity work, speaking, and writing, all in Dustin's honor. Through this, Danny and Kim hope to make a real impact in the world. Maybe up in Heaven Dustin is smiling down on them and feels the warmth and love from all those he left behind. Because he lived life wide open, we can celebrate his life in joy and make our lives better now. The way in which we each live our lives can be a tribute to Dustin if we remember his story. By choosing a designated driver in his honor, or giving to sports scholarships, we can bring peace to his soul, and lift him to greater heights in his heavenly abode.

If that dream of that future where we will be reunited with our loved ones in a tangible way comes true, do you want to explain to God why you were driving drunk and killed people? If that dream of that future lets you converse with those who have passed, would you rather be able to walk up to Dustin in Heaven and say "Thank you for what you and your parents did to warn me. You saved many lives." That dream is real. Few doubt that you will search out your loved ones and even maybe Dustin when the time comes! But until that time, hope rests with you to honor Dustin's life as a small measure of comfort and solace.

EPILOGUE

As I write this epilogue, a yellow butterfly just landed on my window pane and rested a while. I can't help but think it is Dustin's way of saying to me that he is o.k. now. It feels as if he is looking down from heaven and hoping the best for his mom and those who read this book. Commemorating the love Dustin showed us all while he was here enlightened me. His life-song will now echo in the hearts of more than those who knew him while he lived here on earth. Kim is still singing Dustin's life song to others in hopes that it will inspirit citizens to make the right choices in their lives, and lighten the burden of parents who have lost children too soon.

I have seen faith give Kim strength to co-author this book. It deeply touched me the way she remembered the special small fleeting moments of Dustin's days on earth that she now brings to shine in the lives of others. Remembering the essence of who he was, could not fill the hole left in the lives of those who loved Dustin. But the brightness of his life's days will always be there, to shine light on the realization that our life is forever revealing itself to us now. I learned that these flashes of life may seem to last a lifetime, but they pass, and we are left with the lens of love through which we experienced them. That one meeting at a KOA, a place that seemed so ordinary brought me so much. I will never forget how illuminating these brief moments of our lives are. The choices we make every day, every moment profoundly affect the world we leave behind.

If you would like to order a bracelet or donate to the Dustin Ledford Scholarship Fund you may go to Facebook Dustin Ledford Live Wide Open at: https://www.facebook.com/groups/24867291190 2019/

You may also send a petition to strengthen the drunk driving laws in your state by visiting http://www.madd.org/get-involved/take-action/

It takes only two minutes, but the impact can last a lifetime. Those who wish can help MADD eliminate drunk driving by signing up for a MADD Walk event as a walker, team captain, or volunteer. They can even be involved without attending the event, by signing up as a "virtual walker" or making a donation to another walker or team.

Also remember you can donate to the

Dustin Ledford scholarship foundation by visiting Shanes Ribshack. Ten percent of everything you buy on July 10th of every year will go to the scholarship fund.

Thank you for your help in advocating for life-saving legislation in your state. Be sure to visit regularly to see updates on our progress and to support new legislative initiatives.

- See more at:

Tennessee Voices for Victims at:

http://tnvoicesforvictims.org/about/

Tennessee Board of Parole Victim Services at:

https://www.tn.gov/bop/article/bop-victim-services

ABOUT THE AUTHORS

Karen White Porter is a Director of Loga Springs Academy and a Nationally Board Certified Teacher. After graduating from Rutgers University with a Masters Degree in language education, she started teaching children. She has taught at East China Normal University in Shangha, P.R. China, Hofstra University in Hempstead N.Y., Hillside Public Schools in New Jersey, University of Saint Andrews in Saint Andrews Scotland, Belcher Elementary in Clearwater, Florida, The University of South Florida, The State University of Florida, and Loga Springs Academy. She started her own school, Loga Springs Academy, in Gainesville, Florida and became inspired by her students who were self-publishing with Amazon. After working for over 25 years grading students papers, she began a new chapter of her life. She co-authored several books with her daughter about feelings, in her 'Emotatude' series. Her most recent and popular works are How to be Heebie Jeebie Free; What to Do When you Get the Bejeebers Scared Out of You; The Secret of Warm Fuzzies; Picking Up the Pieces of a Kanipshun Fit; and Turtle One and Turtle Two. Her Abby's Read Along Sing Along Picture Books are still used as classroom readers in Pinellas County Schools. She also has developed several other children's' book series.

Kim Mital Ledford is the office manager at Ledford Automotive where she works with her husband Danny. She is the owner of Kim's Embroidery business and has many followers on Pinterest for her creative ideas. She has been awarded the Voices for Victims Award. This organization has the mission to engage and empower victims and citizens in the effort to reduce violent crime. Kim enjoys camping, sewing, crafts, and traveling with her husband. When the weather is just right she and Danny love to ride with the top down on their convertible and enjoy the fresh mountain air and sunshine. She has several Yorkshire terriers and is a member of Waterville Baptist Church. She and her husband Danny still celebrate their love for one another every day. They spoil their granddaughter Serenity and are delighting in seeing her grow up. They continue to be dedicated to teaching young people the dangers of drinking and driving. As we are making the final edits of this book Kim and Danny are being recognized for their works. The Dustin Ledford Scholarship Foundation was awarded the East Tennessee Power of Community Award by the Mothers Against Drunk Driving of Tennessee during a recent celebration of MADD Tennessee's 35th anniversary in Nashville in December of 2015.

Made in United States
North Haven, CT
02 November 2022

26192641R10127